The good book says, "Blessed are they who mourn." The mourning is easier to know than the blessing.

Dr. John Hall has seen enough pain to break anyone's heart.
You would think he would harden to it; but that's not an option for him.
He's too honest.
He's too faithful.
He sees the world as it is.
But read his words with your whole heart and you will hear his unfailing hope for a world as it can be...as it should be.
That hope fills his whole heart.
That hope is what makes him a prophet.

His poetry opens the eyes to the realities of human living when living is less than human.
God has given Dr. John Hall the gift to see beauty where most would miss it;
and the gift to speak truth when most are mute.
Read his poetry and it will break your heart,
but there in the broken places is where his words will whisper blessing.
It makes me wonder if the good book had the good doctor in mind:
Blessed are they who mourn.
He calls his writings snippets.
I call them blessings.

Rev. Tom Are Jr.

This book is for Charlotte, my wife,

Shelly, my daughter,

Kim, my daughter, and her husband John

Brian, my son, and his wife Jamie

Tony and Tori, my grandchildren,

And Samantha, my dog.

For the patients,
Who gave their hope, grace, and messages to be written down.

Thank you to Kelly Howell who helped to bring this book to fruition.

Thank you to Vernon, Sharon, Susanne, Ron, Dorothy, Wayne, Louise, Connie and their families who give me support for the present and hope for the future.

I would particularly like to thank Kimberly Hall-Singleton for her endless work in helping to edit this text in content, thought, and accuracy.

"The really valuable thing in the pageant of human life seems to me not the state but the creative essential individual, the personality: it alone creates the noble and the sublime, while the herd as such remains dull in thought and dull in feeling."

~Albert Einstein

"If God leads the sheep so well, he will also lead a man, he thought, and that made him feel better."

~Paul Coelho from the "The Alchemist"

Prayer of Medicine

I have met the patient

And turned to science for help,

But we were still alone.

Then I turned to God,

And the message was clear.

"Be not afraid,

But have strength,

For you and the patient are one and the same."

Disclaimer

I have been asked if these stories are true. They are
embellished with the aura the story held for me.
While these accounts are, in general, based on
my many years of experience, they are not the story
of any one individual, but a compilation of the variety
of conditions affecting the human condition.
Any resemblance to actual people or circumstances is merely
coincidental.   They are spirits of a place and time where
you can see the reflectance of those around us.
Anyone who thinks they see themselves is imagining.
They are only seeing a mythological piece of themselves
used to make a comment on all of us.

Snippets

Part of the Proceeds from the sale of this book will support the Kansas City Free Health Clinic and Village Presbyterian Church Mission Committee.

Contents

Snippets

Falling Leaves

The colors of autumn,

The pigment of leaves,

Brought on not by cold,

But the lengthening of the night.

There are many patient visits I cannot forget.

But some haunt.

Leave a color change.

Make the world seem different forever.

Social work in America.

Not poverty pay

But it is closer than it should be,

Close enough to take a snippet of your breath away.

What does a social worker do?

Everything.

Snippets

Insurance, lodging, medical bills,

Drug bills, family issues, hospital issues, transportation, affordable food, inheritance

So here is something true and amazing,

Carotenoids and anthocyanins that give the leaf color.

They are there all the time,

They only appear as the chlorophyll is destroyed as the leaf dies.

The green of summer hides the beauty of the fall colors.

Death brings life to the color.

Living ideas,

They may be hidden by ones about to die.

"Do you like being a social worker?"

"I love it." said the young patient before me.

"Got into medical school.

But I wasn't into things."

"But I wasn't into things."

It haunts me still.

Snippets

Is that what medicine has come to?

Or my life, how about my life?

I hope there is hope.

I hope that a cute, pert, serious girl.

Who knows what she is here for.

Doesn't notice that I may not be.

The length of night will lengthen,

The light will shine less long,

The truth will be seen.

Seen by all who look.

So leaves must fall,

The trees will die if they stay,

Freeze to death in the winter.

But the buds, the stems, the branches; they can stand the winter.

They can wait for spring

Ready to help life return,

To be ready,

Snippets

For the leaves of green.

Wait for rebirth,

Wait for the life to surface,

Wait to hide the truth,

Wait for the leaves to change in the fall.

The death of "things"

Revealed her life of service.

And I will see the beauty of the leaves

In a different light this fall.

As the rains of early winter leave a shine of glory

On the wet glistening multicolored coats.

The world will soon be christened by the falling leaves.

"Leg Off On Wednesday"

"Still smoking?" I asked the bedfast patient in room A13.

"I stopped but then I just started again."

"So how many surgical procedures on that leg?"

"Four."

The worst surgery I every assisted on in medical school was a leg amputation.

The surgeon started at the foot.

"No viable tissue here."

Then below the knee.

"Still black."

The mid-thigh.

"We shouldn't have started this."

He died two days later.

I should have stayed an English major.

Smoking is the single largest preventable health tragedy of our time.

It is the largest public health disaster of my lifetime.

Cancer likes smoking, blood vessels don't like smoking.

Habit forming.

Tobacco companies gave it free to soldiers returning from WWII.

Tobacco companies put additives into tobacco to increase addiction.

Snippets

Tobacco companies made up false studies showing tobacco was safe.

There are more smokers in China than people in the United States.

The tobacco stocks are the best.

Lawyers have made their fortunes lying about tobacco.

"I'm a skin doctor and I need to do a biopsy to see what's going on."

But I knew.

"This might hurt."

But I knew.

"Will I lose my leg?" "I don't know."

But I knew.

And all the time, he knew too.

Everyone: nurses, relatives, friends, doctors, said he was a good guy.

Yelp and groan and scream from the patient.

"Its OK doc. Here you are, trying to help."

They call it "trash foot" or Buerger's Disease or in the end, gangrene.

It's embolic, thrombotic, ischemic, necrotic and just simply life-threatening.

Three days later.

Biopsy report: clots, blood vessels disintegrating.

To nurse, "Is he better?"

"Looked worse this morning."

My examination, "He's asleep, I didn't wake him.

Leg is much worse.

What did the surgeon say?"

"Leg off on Wednesday."

"His whole leg looks bad. Below knee surgery? Above knee surgery? It won't work."

"That's what I've been thinking."

"But you have to stop the pain."

"He might die."

"But he might live and he'll die anyway if they don't operate."

It's his fault, he kept smoking

It's God's fault, he invented tobacco.

It's the doctor's fault, he didn't say, "stop or you will lose your leg."

It's the bowling alleys fault, that's where he fell last week and when it started.

It changes nothing.

What changes nothing?

Fault doesn't change, "leg off on Wednesday."

It's too clinical

It's too rational

It's too sad

Snippets

It's too impersonal

It's too inhumane

Too matter of fact

Find the justice,

Find the honor,

Find the glory,

Find the fairness.

It's just not going to be there, it just is what it is.

There is nothing left.

When there is nothing left,

There is only God.

If God is here then God truly is everywhere.

No cross, no Ark of the Covenant, no jihad, no Buddha, no pranava mantra, no prayer beads.

I can't explain, but God looks good all alone sometimes.

As life is in death, as death is in life,

God knew all along.

The surgeon says, "It is his only chance."

But only God can make it holy.

"Leg off on Wednesday."

He knew.

And Still They Come

Today,

 70 people were found in a truck in Austria,

Packed like sardines,

Dead.

Four were children.

No, there were 71,

A one year old girl.

And still they come.

"It is the Muslim hordes,

Soldiers of Allah,

They will ruin us all."

Thus the shrill cries of intolerance rain over the flooding earth.

For they recognize not the shadows of themselves or their God.

Aylan Kurdi, child of Syria,

He died on the beach.

He died for all those who died searching for a place of peace.

He died for those who lived and found a place of peace.

You can never stop them all.

Some will get through

To start new lives.

Maybe they will be your neighbors.

Sixty million people on our planet,

That's how many are trying.

Leaving is better than staying,

It is the story of our age.

They say we cannot help them all.

So it is best to help none.

They say this is not their country.

We were immigrants here first so it is our country."

Thus the shrill cries of intolerance rain over the flooding earth.

For they recognize not the shadows of themselves or their God.

More refugees than God or man have ever seen.

They have no hope where they are,

They only have the hope of something better.

I hope they find it,

If only just a few.

I hope they find it

I hope they find what they are looking for.

Not just the same persecution, starvation, alienation.

This is not new,

One third the population of the country of my wife's ancestors, the Irish,

tried crossing the Atlantic in one year.

The Atlantic and the Mediterranean can be burial grounds of equal import.

And still they come.

"The Irish hordes would ruin us all,

They were soldiers for the Pope,

Our country would not survive."

Thus the shrill cries of intolerance rain over the flooding earth.

For they see not the shadows of themselves or their God.

The disinherited of the world,

Where will we leave them?

Where will we find them?

Somewhere.

Who are these people, the sixty million?

They are just people you know.

They are all just doing that we would do.

They will never go home.

Snippets

Will we save their lives?

Will we be one with them?

Will they be one with us?

Who will be watching?

The masses that arrive on our shores,

The refuse of every war and natural disaster,

The Jews, the Palestinians, the Christians, the Russians, the Slavs, the Germans,

The Muslims, the Somali, the Huguenots, the Acadians, the Vietnamese, the Chinese, the Pilgrims of all races who have fled from place to place.

What will they see?

The most strongly guarded border in the world.

Mexico and the United States

6.9 billion dollars per year.

It doesn't work.

They say, "use armed drones at the border."

They say, "build a better wall."

They say, "spend more money on border security."

They say, "100% apprehension at the border."

And insanity takes the day.

Thus the shrill cries of intolerance rain over the flooding earth.

For they see not the shadows of themselves or their God.

And still they come.

We can never build a wall high enough,

We can never ship them all back from where they came.

We can kill some of them and watch others die.

But they will still come, the masses, they are just us of another time,

When the last of the people of the earth line up to find another planet,

When the meteor hits or the sun is dying.

I hope they give us a place in the line

and give us the same hope we gave them.

But maybe not.

Until death has died.

Until new life no longer restores the old.

Until there is no mankind left to search for the promise of a new life.

And still they come.

Bleeding Heart

Sometimes the best things are in corners.

Where two walls meet

Things get squared off there

And made straight.

Her name had to be Tammy.

You know, sweet, perky, poised,

but, most of all, just fun.

A visit to my dermatology office was always refreshing.

Her son was the patient.

Psoriasis, thick scales on a red base

Elbows, knees, scalp,

But pretty easy to control.

The repertoire between mother and son.

The best and most entertaining ever.

Their love had shown unrelenting.

Best friends forever.

I would have scheduled them,

just to see their act.

Even if there were no flakes of skin.

You can't have too much Tammy.

The boy had muscular dystrophy,

The kind that leads to death.

She was a single mom with one son.

But she was still Tammy.

Her news today.

It broke my heart.

Breast cancer, metastatic.

She was still Tammy.

"I can't die first.

He would be put in an institute.

He would die alone."

Still Tammy.

Short story.

She died first.

Her son died alone in a sterile room,

It was just as she had feared.

In the Vaihingen Concentration Camp during the Holocaust,

One of the highest mortality rates of any such camp.

And still they performed the Passover Sader,

The Nazis thought they needed the flour to make paste to put up Hitler posters.

Would you like to fall down and cry to the stars?

I would.

Could you bleed from your heart in protest of fate?

I can't.

But someday I will

I will be looking up from the ground

And bleeding my heart out

Next to a mother and her son.

There is a great reddish blue, purple door on the time warp.

It is automatic don't you know.

It opens in a blink with a blink of the eye.

The room before you is filled with corners.

That's when I learned about corners.

They are closed on two sides

But open on two sides

And there is the rub.

They collect what the winds bring in.

Snippets

They catch memories both good and bad

The dust of our thoughts

The things carried in time.

In the corners are also the great pairings of the past.

The back and forth of the great double combos of our lives.

They are above all entertaining and clever.

Aristotle and student, Laurel and Hardy, Abbott and Costello, Burns and Allen,

Job and God, Jesus and the disciples.

And in one of the corners, the farthest from the door, which is the best place to be,

There you can see Tammy and her son.

No combination is better than this.

Their banter is above reproach.

I can faintly hear Tammy through the haze of chemotherapy,

And her son through the heavy thought of losing her forever.

But don't let their handicaps fool you.

There is great theater and conversation to be had.

I wonder why I always think about Tammy.

Why would I break my heart over and over again?

Why would I want to be a bleeding heart?

Snippets

Because she is still Tammy.

Dearest God, she is still dearest Tammy.

Missing the Choir

You have to do it.

Step off the cliff into the black.

Black, the absence of all colors

Black, the choice of the entire universe and its sisters.

They stand two rows deep.

Their leader can be anyone.

As long as they are mothers, daughters, aunts, grandmothers, granddaughters.

Any Kenyan mavoureen of the village, from very young to very old.

No instruments but the voice,

Nothing to hear but the plaintive wail of the leader.

Nothing to spoil the first clear sound that pierces the night

And even the gentle desert breeze stops to listen.

Who will give the note of perfect pitch in the pitch blackness?

No man-made device is available in a poor village.

Even the wild dogs hold their notes.

It is the scent of the veldt that gives the absolute tone.

The moon and stars are the spotlight, the red parched earth is the stage.

They sing until they can no longer.

Always another to take their place.

Then do they miss a beat? Never.

They are slaves no more.

They took the religion of their captors

And melded it into the red dust of their ancestors

And they sing for heaven and all to hear.

So the people of the Serengeti should not be singing.

They are the poorest of the poor,

Their government is the most corrupt,

But sing oh God, sing they will.

The origin of man has been discovered here

We will all carry the DNA of the tribes of Kenya and Eritrea forever,

And with it their music

Their voices, their rhythm, their song.

Just as the first rays of sun

Lit the way for man's first steps to cover the planet,

Snippets

East Africa's first song

Paved the way for all of man's voices to follow.

The scene is the high desert at darkness.

The audience, wild dogs, snakes, weaver birds, chickens, goats, cattle,

The thorn bushes, the dying corn, the pigeon peas,

The people of the village and their God, the object of every verse.

The concert ends when it ends.

Dawn is the final curtain on holidays.

I don't understand Swahili,

But the scene and sounds lift me up as no other.

Ignorance of the native tongue is best.

It leaves me with the transcendence of the song.

The music becomes not Muslim, Christian, Jew, Hindu, Buddhist but in search of God,

They are all of the above, singing above it all.

There is something primordial about a human voice in the night.

The Africans of the East have carried it through the void since man's first cry.

They will carry it on into the ages beyond.

No joy will be enshrined above the call of these sirene.

Singing daily in my brain,

That is where I will hear them again.

I cannot take the choir with me.

But I will always be missing the choir.

My sister had been on the phone before this Kenyan trip.

"We have a small family, massacre at Garissa,

Boco Haram is on the loose.

You are taking my granddaughter!"

Two separate weekends of tears and pleading.

Brother-in-law joins the lament.

"I don't usually ask much of you, John,

But I am asking you not to go,"

The dark of East Africa is little changed from the time of the Massai.

It is easy for the eyes of the natives.

My pupils strain to catch the light,

But it is not enough.

But the music I catch.

Not a television, radio or I-pad for the having

So the entertainment void must be filled

Practice is every night from birth to death.

Even in the darkness you imagine their clothes.

Every color of the rainbow and beyond,

Their everyday dress

Is all the glory the eye can hold.

I could have stayed at home

I could have missed the "eine klein en nacht music" of Africa

But then I would be writing of something different,

Maybe of lesser things and lesser sounds.

The leader sang the main line

The choir answered in perfect time

All was memorized

All was mesmerizing.

Theirs' is the voice of the cave,

The volcano, the grasslands,

The birth, the children,

The old and the legacy all man has left behind.

The lion, the wildebeest, the umbrella trees,

The seeds of the plants we now grow,

The same droplets of water that fall on us now,

Have all gloried in these voices before us.

No space on earth is darker than East Africa.

You are swallowed whole by the dark.

You catch your breath from black nothingness

Your body is gone; your soul is left alone.

The song and the night clamor to dominate,

But the night succumbs.

It joins the chorus.

They are as one.

Their dance you cannot see is always with their song.

Their feet, their hands,

Their hips, their heads,

All tell the story.

They sway and dance to the words.

Their ages mix as the sounds become one age only.

The age of celebration, joy, and of the mystic.

But most of all the age of praise.

I could have succumbed.

To malaria, snake bite, senseless violence.

I could have matched the fear of my family

But then I would be missing my benediction.

Missing the chance to hear angels on earth,

Missing the chance to honor the maker of us all,

Missing the reason we are on earth,

Missing the choir.

Cecil Willy

Cecil Willy is God.

He never told me he was,

And I never asked him.

But he's God alright.

I recognized him,

But not at first.

He was big and midnight black

I have never seen him cry

But he had plenty of reason to weep

About 12 months ago is as good an estimate as any

He started to get deep undermining draining abscesses

Snippets

They hurt like the devil.

They started in his groin and then his armpits and then his scalp,

And then the worst ones of all on his face.

It has a name—the triad of dissecting cellulitis of the scalp,

Cystic acne, and hidradinitis suppurativa.

We dermatologists can name anything on the skin.

The name is not, however, important.

He lost his job-can't drain pus all day on most jobs.

He lost his wife-hard to love someone with yellow oozing all over everything.

He never had any health insurance.

He is an American.

Lived in Kansas City all his life-he was born there.

So he decided to make an appointment at the big city hospital downtown.

They would see anybody there,

I guess even God

But they were seven months behind on an appointment

Too many people on Medicaid or Medicare or without health insurance

So Cecil Willy got much worse

He got thick, deep, debilitating scars

He lost his friends and became depressed

He wasn't much of a man any more,

You know, with pain and drainage all the time and looking a little scary.

So this is where I come in,

God finally slipped in with an appointment at the free health clinic.

He looked pretty sad and his story was on the unpleasant side of things.

"We can make you better,

But it will be slow and the scars are here to stay."

Cecil Willy had no comment.

He had a sort of glassy look

If you could find any look under his swollen face.

That whole left cheek was a bulging, red mass, very tender and is hard to forget.

So I haven't forgotten it.

And who could forget a visit from God, anyway.

So three months of steroids, antibiotics, retinoids

And Cecil Willy was left only with the horrific disfigurement,

But his disease was gone—no pain, no pus, no swelling.

"We've almost tapered you off your meds so I won't need to see you again."

That's when I found out he was God

"I'm not going anywhere, I'll see you every month."

"Until one of us dies, you mean."

"No, every month."

Snippets

And here is the thing,

You know, the thing,

The reason I wrote this,

So you could meet God too.

Cecil Willy comes to the clinic at least once a month.

He actually comes everyday.

He comes unannounced in the middle of my dreams.

Sometimes he even comes at night when I'm awake.

He comes when I need him the most, when I'm in deep depression.

It's when my pills don't work and I need extra help

From the pain, the loneliness, the fear of failure,

The knowing I made the wrong turn.

The knowing that I didn't do what was right.

His scars are weird

Like I've never seen before

The edges fold up in little rolls that you can peel off his skin.

He peels them off sometimes.

Sometimes I peel them off.

It doesn't seem to hurt.

Still a little on the unusual side of things is that I found out I knew him before.

Before high school

When they made jokes of my fat

Snippets

My diarrhea

My falling trying to catch a ball in right field

My brother said, "you should get up and chase the ball."

"I knew that."

My failure to climb the rope in gym class.

In medical school when my anatomy professor said,

"I can see you're really not serious about medical school."

In my in internship, I had even met him several times,

Coughing up phlegm on the pulmonary ward,

In DT's on psych rounds,

When the leukemia of no return diagnosis hit the fan in heme/onc clinic.

Later, not long before my dad died he was the orderly with the round black face,

Who smiled at me and my father in the small low bed

When they were trying to decide on the feeding tube.

Later, when my wife said,

"You've got to get help.

It's got to stop.

You promise you'll change but you don't.

You're changing for the worse."

And later when I'm slipping, slipping away.

There's that funny Cecil Willy smile.

Just when I think he's gone,

He's not. He says he loves me.

God's like that or should I say Cecil's like that.

You know, Cecil Willy.

You know Cecil Willy?

Non sum dingus.

Small Kenya

Kenya is a country in Africa.

Not that small really,

But compared to Africa as a whole, it is small.

Went to Kenya,

A minister and some friends and once my great niece.

It is very scenic there with Mount Kilamanjaro and all.

But that's not why we went.

We went to start a medical clinic and see patients.

So we did.

Sans indoor plumbing, electricity, running water.

You don't need heating or cooling

Warm in the day and cool at night.

We trained a nurse to stay at the clinic and sleep there.

She had a doctor drive down from Nairobi for difficult cases.

She could call an ambulance.

It was 7 hours one way if a really difficult case or a patient dying.

It is no small distance.

Hundreds of patients day two,

A child not too small for his age of ten.

But for the human race as a whole, he was small.

He had problems.

Covered with blisters.

Headache.

Stiff neck.

Painful abdomen.

Exhaustion in his small eyes.

No lab to culture or biopsy blisters.

No equipment for a lumbar puncture.

No place for an abdominal x-ray.

"I think he has chickenpox." to Swahili nurse interpreter.

"I think he might have meningitis or hepatitis." I had seen chickenpox do just that.

"We need acyclovir."

Snippets

Nurse, "we have none."

"Get Pastor David.

He's from here and maybe he knows a medication cache somewhere."

From Pastor, "None here.

I'll leave for Nairobi now but won't be back until morning at best."

"Get out, go. This kid may die."

David and I liked each other in kind of a foreign way.

Through interpreter, "Can her son come back tomorrow."

"She said she had planned on coming back tomorrow."

"Because?"

"She says that is the day God said he would save her son.

So she knew she would have to come back."

"God knows this?"

"That is what she says."

"Poor interpreting, nurse."

"I don't think so Doc."

Al shabaab within 100 miles of our voices is killing mothers, fathers, and children

They are so busy doing what they say the will of God tells them.

They say they can hear God.

They surely need a rest from their draconian deeds.

The day is warmer than usual with little breeze.

I wish they would start the long trek over the fissured rock of the volcanic plain.

Under the umbrella trees, past the fields of pigeon peas, over the lion's land,

Past the kudu, and the elephant taking its red dust shower,

And the quiet buffalo lounging in the blood of the glowing dusk.

Through the sienna sludge of the slums in Kibera.

They could see the God they claimed to hear.

He's coming tomorrow.

This from someone who should know,

The mother of child who may be dying.

It would be a small gesture.

Not many foreign press.

But such a chance to see God.

The Swahili are the largest tribe in Kenya and the country is 80% Christian.

They were not always Christian but very religious.

They, like many, combine their old beliefs with the new.

They even have two names: their Kenyan names and their Christian names.

For them it is not incompatible.

So the exact God who had proclaimed this state of affairs was not identified.

It is possible, of course, that there is only one God.

Even so, God had a lot of nerve talking to this mother with such authority.

"She has more faith than I do."

I had a kind of foreign relationship with God.

"I have cried about this later."

One little kid is so small compared to the tribes of Kenya.

Even smaller to the tribes of the world.

Does anyone really care?

I doubt it.

Do you think God really cared?

I doubt it.

Don't be shocked, we all doubt it.

But that mother didn't.

Poor religion.

Belief is small compared to life.

But I was going to be sure to see if God showed.

3:00 AM. Nurse, "Wake up David's back!"

Did he get the medicine?"

"He's gone again, we'll see tomorrow."

I asked a Kenyan nurse practitioner who made the grueling trip from Nairobi.

She came to help at the clinic.

I couldn't help myself so I had to ask,

"Why are all Kenyan women so beautiful?"

"Because we were made in the image of God."

Oh yes, God, I forgot to tell you about God.

God never came.

Neither did al shabaab.

David brought the medicine.

We all stood there to watch the boy take the first few pills.

I learned months later when I was back in Kansas City,

The boy had done fine with a full recovery.

No sequalae.

Either I had over diagnosed or we had gotten lucky.

No difference,

He was OK.

So the Hyrax sits and suns on a rock all day.

Seemingly oblivious to the dangers around her.

She must keep her body temperature up.

She has done it that way for centuries.

She sees the sun go up every day over the equator at 6:00 AM.

She sees the sun go down every day over the equator at 6:00 PM,

She doesn't seem bored.

She seems to be enjoying the constant change in the scenery.

And the sameness of the weather, year after year.

She is not Kosher according to Leviticus but she doesn't seem to care.

She can brag that her lineage is that of the elephant.

But she is small and that is satisfactory.

I wish I could sit there with her.

And see what goes on during the rainy season and the drought.

Maybe she is waiting just like me.

To see if God shows up.

To tell the Muslims, the Christians, the people who murder.

The dead, the mourning.

To tell them it will be alright.

To tell them we all are small.

We all are small Kenya.

God is small too.

Just like us.

He went to Kenya too.

But he is so small we didn't see him.

Weakness

Kenya, the poorest place on earth, there is one last patient to see.

Tall, elderly, man, mostly blind, with a stiff limp, shuffles in.

No teeth in his head, he leads in the patient, a girl.

And slumps in a chair with legs, without a bend, stretched forward.

Snippets

The strange couple.

Both black as night.

With a certain kindness in the older named Subira.

And the younger stands at attention named Kibwe.

Kibwe opened her mouth as wide as she could.

It was what she did when she met a doctor and she had met many.

Interpreter, "Doctor Hall wants to see your skin.

Do you itch?"

"Yes madame, I itch.

Will you make it stop?"

"Yes it will stop,

But it may come back again."

In an orphanage for AIDS, scabies spreads fast.

Seven year old children can pick it up quickly,

From other children, from health care workers.

From those seeking sexual favors.

I can't get her out of my mind.

Or out of my heart. Parents died of HIV.

Her picture keeps showing up on my computer.

Mouth agape, eyes closed tight, as if to please any giver of hope.

Filled with weakness.

Knees quaking.

Stomach knotting.

I feel things begin to spin.

I wanted to grab her frail body.

And surround her with my arms.

She could nestle against my chest.

And I could whisper it was going to be all right at last.

I would let her sleep secure,

And we would drift away.

Her AIDS would move to my blood.

Her scabies would move to my skin.

It would be ok.

Theresia, my nurse, could run the clinic.

Charlotte, my wife, could run the family.

I could just hold Kibwe.

Thought we saw an archangel,

Metatron? Israfel? Azreal? Michael? Gabriel?

No, it was one just for us.

It was our very own.

Above the stars and the clouds.

Above the universe.

To the next universe.

We would fold into one.

When we broke apart,

She could have what was left of my life of privilege,

And I could finish out her life of suffering.

It would be something to make us both worthwhile after all.

And that little piece of love that we made,

It could just float to infiniteness.

To join all the love.

All the love in God's endless realm.

The Marine

I am not a Marine.

I have never been in the military.

I have never risked my life to defend democracy.

I have never served my country as a soldier.

But on a cold November day,

We all joined the Marines.

We all became the guardians of our destiny.

We all had a chance to see what the final sacrifice can be.

It was cold.

It was, after all, November in the land of the brave and the home of the free.

The Marine in question was spending his time before the end of the year,

The way he had spent it for years.

Standing in a WalMart,

Collecting Toys for Tots,

In the uniform of his country,

With duty written on his face.

I have always enjoyed breaking rules.

I like getting away with things.

Not for any particular purpose.

Just because I thought it was just.

No real big rules,

Just minor ones.

Not those that would result in time in prison.

Just those that would make a point and infuriate others.

It is not a good habit.

It has lost some friends.

It has made some people think ill of me.

But some things you can't help.

I have a big mouth.

My minister once said of me.

"He is apt to give you his opinion,

Even if you don't want it."

This is one of the many comments about me that I love.

I love the sincerity with which it was spoken.

I love the person who spoke it.

It is what I call a reverse compliment.

To take the unpopular side,

Is a genetic aberration I own and have perfected.

I will be better from now on

But not today.

So there is a rule at WalMart that states,

"No solicitation can be done inside of any WalMart Store."

I like rules like this.

Snippets

They are easy to break with no jail time usually required.

The marine, unlike me, was not a rule breaker.

So after years of his end of the year charity work,

When he was asked, rudely it was reported, to leave the warmth of the WalMart and step outside,

He did the unthinkable, he stepped outside.

No protest, total restraint, polite approaching painful.

The Marines are a few good men.

I am probably not a few good men.

I sometimes wish that I could be but I am not.

So WalMart sells a lot of crap in very large quantities.

They are friendly, they have greeters.

They give people jobs of exceptionally low pay

And seem to not always be fair to women.

No one is perfect.

I am not perfect.

WalMart is not perfect.

The marine was not perfect.

But the marine was much closer to perfect than most.

But WalMart is in business to make money.

Snippets

To do this they sell cheap shit.

Many local stores throughout our country know how good WalMart does business.

That is why they don't have a business anymore.

WalMart keeps salaries down.

They think the minimum wage should be kept down.

They keep benefits down.

Their stock and profits have recently been down.

Down may be the new up at WalMart.

But the marine is the new up in my book.

The marine is outside in the freezing cold, standing up.

On the moral scale he is most decidedly very up.

So now the Marine stands outside in the deep freeze of winter.

He collects Toys for Tots.

He says it is not about him but about the kids.

WalMart, quite by surprise, has made a poor business decision.

There is an art gallery of great repute in Arkansas.

It is invented by the great WalMart clan.

My friends take bus tours to see the glory of the canvasses.

They come back muttering and sputtering with praise.

I have heard, although not seen,

42

Snippets

There are no paintings of failed shops

Or lives ruined

By WalMart greed.

I hope the marine, who is getting up in years,

Is warm this winter and many winters to follow.

I think this is unlikely,

But I hope for it anyway.

I don't know if the marine is an art enthusiast,

I know he likes children.

I know he could teach WalMart about marketing.

Breaking rules can sell a lot of crap.

Something

So I am in pain virtually all the time.

And it is virtually a secret.

No friends know.

My wife and my kids know a little.

Snippets

My doctors know a little.

They are helpful

But not much.

Some are compassionate, but not much.

So medicine has a pain gauge.

On a scale of 10 the worst, we give it a grade from 1 to 10.

I'm not that good at math,

So I don't do the scale very often, even at night.

The nights are the worst.

It's too bad because I love the night.

I know this because sometimes

When I am at a "1" the night sings to me.

I can't keep it a secret from my dreams.

Rats gnaw on my feet.

I limp with a draining sore that will not heal.

I see endless doctors with no help to be found.

A new dream.

I cut my foot.

God sees it and decides to make it worse.

She sews the sinews with no anesthetic.

Now the real kick.

I thank God for the favor done me.

I give her the thumbs up

And She returns the same sign.

I awake.

The pain is real

And so is the thanks.

How can that be?

No one should know the pain but me.

Or else it defines me.

Defines me as pain.

That is not who I am.

Today on my desk lays the most recent copy of the NEJM.

The New England Journal of Medicine,

The world's most prestigious medical journal.

Today is 2/10/16.

The Journal says we have the lowest life expectancy of all the world's industrialized nations.

Over 100% of this anomaly is accounted for by 3 factors.

Death by firearms, motor vehicle accidents,

Snippets

And drug abuse.

Prescription drug abuse is exploding in America.

15 million prescription drug abusers in 2014.

Most of these drugs are narcotics.

First given for pain relief.

The medical students

They say they know what doctors will prescribe narcotics

The addicted know too.

If not, there is always the pain clinic, narcotics handed out like candy

So I would like to have no pain.

But it is not to be.

Not to be for the last 9 years.

So I live from 4 to 6 on the famous pain scale.

A few sevens but no zeros.

But I have learned a separate life where I live at zero.

I live a zero in the arms of the edge of freedom.

Freedom gives you everything you want.

Freedom gives you life.

Freedom gives you healing.

It is something that gives you the light of tomorrow.

It is something and it has a name.

She named it for us all.

It replaces the names for pain,

The names for pain killers,

The names for abuse.

I am not named for pain.

I was told by my by minister

That She knows all our names.

Mine is Freedom and that is something.

Perfect

So I like pickles

Very much

Sweet, sour

There actually is a sweet and sour.

Water, vinegar, sugar, salt and spices.

You can pickle any vegetable or fruit.

Snippets

My sister makes the best.

Cucumbers from her garden picked with love.

I can eat a jar at one sitting

It is something about the crunch

The cold tongue shattering taste

And the pucker the pickle packs.

It is distinctly not healthy.

I mean sugar and salt.

The enemies of diabetes and hypertension all in one.

But that increases the thrill of the pickle.

Medical school was hard.

English majors don't take much science.

And I didn't take any but the basics.

Not a recommended Pre-Med curriculum.

So I thought I would write to relax.

But it wasn't relaxing.

Here is the rub,

Nothing had been done to write about.

Fiction or nonfiction experience can come in handy.

Snippets

Little material to process.

Life had been good.

Not eventful.

So Elgin Miller was a patient at the county hospital.

He was in heart failure.

No heart transplants when I was in medical school.

He was on an inexorable decline.

I was the Med student assigned to follow him.

To follow a patient to me was a kind of journey.

Medical problems are interesting.

The patient is more interesting.

Elgin was a farmer in the age of farming.

He was one of the persons you could talk to forever.

About anything.

No critic, or man of great opinion but he could listen.

So we were friends on the first encounter.

He liked to talk about farming,

Weather, people in the hospital,

Family, friends, every object and stantion in the stillness or the wind.

Our ramblings led to getting a little behind on other pursuits.

49

Snippets

The relationship really took off when I found out Elgin liked pickles.

Now we had arrived

At almost the perfect relationship.

"They told me I can't eat pickles,

And I love pickles."

I was sad

But spoke not a word.

So all this happened before:

I met my wife,

Discovered my brother,

Knew one sister made pickles.

And before:

One sister lost a son

I became a MD, met my patients, made good friends,

And joined a church with a minister of love.

That is my excuse

For doing nothing.

Now I would know what to do

Without hesitation.

Go to Safeway.

Find a jar with the largest pickles.

Make sure I could see through the glass!

Have a little sprig of dill in the jar!

Take them to Elgin's room.

Sit together and eat every single pickle!

We would savor something that was absolutely perfect.

What's Going On

He wore a sweater,

But in my memory it seemed like it was spring.

He was cute.

Of course, I thought my 3 year-old grandson looked cute.

I wanted to wait in line to talk to the minister.

I did this even though the squiggles had attacked my progeny who was getting loud.

It was something I had promised myself I would do.

I wanted him to know.

"This is my grandson, Tony.

Tony, this is the man who keeps me going".

"Quite the contrary is true," from the man before me.

What does he mean? What's going on?

I thought about it later.

He must mean I support the church.

But that means nothing.

He supports my life.

My grandson is now ten.

I am 68.

My minister has no age.

He is of the ageless.

It is not winter now.

It is the soggy, burning summer skies that let you know.

No sweaters now for sure.

Too hot to stand in line.

He nods his head and smiles.

His silver hair shines like white taffy.

His eyes are merely eyes.

But his smile lights up the shallow sidewalk.

Snippets

No religion for me.

God does not talk to me.

But sometimes I feel Her.

All because of Tom, the preacher.

I just want to have some peace.

You must have wanted that sometimes

Just a piece of peace to quiet life a little.

Sometime when it is cool in the early evening.

So he never tells you what to feel.

He never tells you not to be loud.

He never tells you to see God all the time.

He just wants me to ask, "What's going on?"

There are times the weight of it all is on the shoulders of the sky.

When you just want to stand up and fly away.

And lift the burdens from your fellowman.

And claim that we are all at peace at last.

"If I understand the text," he says.

It is about holding on to love

From them to us, from here to there,

From Her to everything.

Now there is a saying about God.

"If there wasn't one we would have to invent one."

My grandkids say, "Good night, Grandpa. I love you."

And we invented Her.

It is sometimes too hot to stand in line.

But it is never too hot for Tom's smile and a nod.

It is never too hot for me to hold Tony with his prickly wool sweater.

It is never too hot to ask, "What's going on?"

Long after I am gone,

The messages of love that lift to the skies from the leaders of faith

Will still be lingering in the air over all of life.

Mountains

There are mountains of data.

Maybe too much.

We have no space for it all.

We have to choose what to keep.

Snippets

The mountains of western Kansas

Are not mountains at all,

Just gigantic rolling mounds,

Covered with grass.

You could fit a lot of data in those wide valleys,

And have a little left over for scenery.

But just like every place else,

You would run out of space eventually.

Jacob Sterling studied hard.

He was a superior medical student.

He, of course, wanted to do research in cardiology.

The specialists of the center of the soul, the heart.

He spent as many parts of his training, as feasible, some at my hospital.

In the presence of the esteemed doctor's of the heart.

He needed recommendation's to get a residency to become one of these esteemed.

Cardiology: long hours, lower pay in research, high expectation.

Jacob spent a month with me in my dermatology office.

Thought he'd pick up a few skin nuggets.

To help him later on.

It had been a long Monday.

"Can I talk to you?

The big cheese in cardiology let me help him with their new drug study.

A patient died, and I was told to just let it slip out of the data.

To keep it out of the study.

Not important.

No one would know.

It would mess things up."

I let it pass by without much comment.

I could have told him that we all stand on a little sand.

But this was a lot of sand with no grass so I let it go.

I let it fade away and missed a good teaching moment.

The Flint Hills of Kansas hold the secrets of the heart.

There are places in the grass where the arrowheads are found.

Sharp reminders of who was there first.

Not Jacob from Wakeeney, Kansas but the man of red from Asia, Major.

You could learn from the feathered forbearers about pride.

About how the spirits owned the holy land,

About the way you kill an enemy by cutting out his heart.

The vanquished would live forever with their missing heartless soul.

56

American Indians did not make good slaves.

Too many suicides when their culture fell apart.

Still happens today.

White men don't understand it.

The hordes of immigrants left their homes and replaced the Indians.

They did not see God in the prairies.

Their places of worship were built by the vanishing forests.

They used up and sent home the spoils of the earth.

They thought they had escaped famine, poverty, war.

The hope they brought with them,

The hope they took from others,

It fell apart.

The cathedrals built by the Europeans are mostly empty now.

The grasslands of the Flint Hills are mostly abandoned.

The research laboratories beg for doctors and money.

Jacob Sterling changed to emergency medicine with no plans for research.

Broken promises was the diagnosis.

The Indian, the pioneers, and Jacob Sterling,

They all had maladies of the heart.

It just came in different ways.

Buried in those mountains of data,

Lost forever in the vast canyons of paper,

There might be some information,

That might save more than a few hearts.

They wait.

Worship houses, Lakota lands, and NIH labs.

A kid with a big dream,

Jacob Sterling.

Put on Indian red, medical white, or holy purple.

You are not alone.

Don't give up.

Climb those mountains, Jacob Sterling!

Episcopalian

Episcopalian I am not.

But I love to say the word.

Church by bishops.

God in symbols.

I sell them short, I know.

Just like Bishop Beach.

I sold him short.

He holds me a bit long for who I really am.

No one holds cancer short.

Nor did the good bishop.

He knew it resided on his noble nose.

Multiple men heaped in robes of medicine disagreed.

I disagreed, my nurse disagreed.

The Bishop's wife was quiet.

The Bishop was not quiet.

"It is there, the cancer on my nose."

"I see nothing dear sir.

Nor does the community of medicine.

Nothing to see.

Nothing to biopsy.

Who is filling your mind with this notion?

"My God."

Difficult argument there.

Where to biopsy to find the proof? "Where it sits upon my face."

"Point the way."

He did.

The knife cut a slab of nose for the lab.

The lab said it was cancer quite deep.

Bishop Beach is short of himself with less of a nose than before,

But he has a nose, nonetheless.

I am short of myself and little believe in God,

But now I have belief, nonetheless.

Bishop Beach said, "You are a troubled man."

His hand upon my head, "Let us pray,".

Alas, I am troubled still.

But the Bishop cared enough to try.

Bishop Beach is not a practitioner of medicine.

I am not a cleric of the church.

I am just a man who tries to be a good physician.

Bishop Beach is just a man who tries to be a good Episcopalian.

Really

I don't really believe in miracles.

Neither does God.

For it is just another day's work.

Not really a miracle at all.

Mrs. Resolve is not really a miracle pusher either.

But the idea of miracles keeps rearing up in her thoughts these days.

One thing for sure,

She is a planner.

But plans and miracles can get entangled,

So I have learned.

You are seldom something you had planned.

You may think you are but most of the time you made it up.

Making things up takes the sting out of things.

It makes you think you know what you are doing.

It makes it seem like you planned it.

You didn't of course.

The winters have changed in Kansas City.

Snippets

No more 6-inch snow falls that melt 4 months later.

It is not necessarily an improvement.

Will still get ice, sleet, and some white stuff.

The weather actually has changed fast.

So Mrs. Resolver noticed things were changing.

Slow at first.

But then just like her winters things really changed fast.

Not feeling too good in the evenings.

A little gasp when inhaling in the morning.

Seemed to be a step behind her normal self.

So she decided on a trip to a miracle medicine man.

Many mystery tests later

And a biopsy or two.

Now we have grim news.

Uterine cancer metastatic to lungs.

Prognosis was more grimness.

Massive debilitating chemotherapy

That might give 3 months of excruciating life

Or maybe better, do nothing.

Snippets

So I have lost faith in man and in God.

I have done it many times in many places.

I lost it in Oklahoma City, Columbine, New York, Tucson, and Sandy Hook.

No reason to find it with Ms. Resolver.

They were planners in those cities too.

Mrs. Resolver had a plan to see her granddaughter graduate.

It was a high school graduation.

A modest plan I thought.

It was in 4 months.

One extra month beyond the chemotherapy she decided to never take.

Chemo was never really on the radar.

You can't attend graduation vomiting and rolled up in the fetal position.

She did go to graduation.

Other events included; First granddaughter-one year later,

First grandson-two years later,

Fifty fifth wedding anniversary- last week.

It has been over 5 years since her predicted demise.

She has more plans for the future of course.

My plan is to see her again for her 6 month check-up.

You see, I'm trying to be more of a planner myself.

The crackle of the table paper whispers as she sits.

The glint in her eyes sparkles in the bright exam light.

Her brown curly hair has a halo effect.

She chats casually with a hint of not enough oxygen.

She is very matter of fact.

Her story has left me less so.

Not a lot for her oncologist to say, he just opens his hands in disbelief.

Not a lot for me to say either but, "really?" Really

Enough

Robert Savage had had enough.

Enough pain.

Enough false hope.

Enough surgery.

His son was a friend of my son,

In seventh grade,

Nice kid,

I think.

Robert Savage was given the best therapy of the time for his acne.

His parents would never let their son scar.

They were diligent.

They made sure Robert kept his appointment for X-ray therapy.

Radiation therapy in this country was all the rage,

It worked for everything,

Asthma, hay fever, warts, skin cancer but most of all for acne.

In the early and mid 1900's it was a dermatologist's dream therapy.

Safe, effective, and painless.

Required numerous visits so a money-maker.

It was new medicine.

It made us look up to date and scientific, like a laser.

In 1977, I still knew a doctor who used it routinely.

That stopped completely of course in the 1980's when we knew it caused bad things like cancer.

We began to save it for bad things only, like cancer.

Bad things in the long run.

But not in the short run.

In the short run it was the magic bullet.

They say that before they tested the first atomic bomb,

At White Sands in the desert,

Snippets

That at least one man of physics thought,

"What if the nuclear fission never stops?"

For Mr. Savage it never did.

"The skin never forgets the radiation it gets."

A quote from Gordon Sauer MD.

The dermatologist's dermatologist.

The land never forgets either.

Those of us downwind from the nuclear tests sites

Still have increase risk for various cancers.

It lasts so long it might as well be forever.

So the skin on Mr. Savage's face

Was the road map left by Einstein and Bohr.

The more cancer we found,

The more disfigurement we created.

"Sideways" my father would say as a euphemism for suicide.

Since some believe you end below in Hell

And others believe all go above to Heaven,

Maybe it really is sideways.

Different ways to go sideways.

Mr. Savage did the hardest one.

He stopped treating his skin cancers.

The result was catastrophe.

When your skyscraper building is on fire,

You can burn slowly,

Or jump to certain death.

Mr. Savage decided not to jump but to burn slowly from the fires of his childhood.

I have heard that science will save us all.

I pray everyday that it is spoken by someone who knows.

Someone who thinks faith and luck are

Just faith and luck.

They think we don't need God.

Mr. Savage must have wondered.

Wondered if we need only science.

Wondered what these people of science would have said.

Were they there when the grisly ulcers and pain and weakness took their toll?

Were they, the men of science, there at the funeral?

Were they who thought x-ray was the answer of answers?

Acne for cancer was a trade?

I know,

Snippets

All you can do is try.

But some days,

We have had enough.

Enough of science and its miracles.

Can you hear us?

Can anyone hear us?

Can anything hear us?

We have had enough.

Science says it will get it right next time.

Next time,

I think I will take my chances with God.

Over Here

Ms. Gravitas

A patient of mine forever (well, forty years)

You know time.

She certainly did at 87 years.

"Nurse, what is the problem?"

"Bump on chest but it is gone."

It was hard to see Ms. Gravites over the computer screen.

She had all her faculties.

If she said it was gone, it was gone.

"Code for that?"

"1323334. Damn those codes."

 Damn these new fees. Not enough."

Too much loss of being grateful for what I have. Too much.

"Nice to see you. Have a great week."

"Did you ask me, why I am here?"

"Nurse said a bump and it's gone.

Later, say hi to the better half."

And all the problems of the world are now explained.

The least of these, the stranger, the second great commandment,

I have all fully just taught these to you.

I don't have time to explain in all to you.

I am busy. Busy beyond belief.

Morey Gravitis was not a rich man, nor was he poor.

His health was very rich for his poor age of 93.

But it's hard to be rich and poor at the same time.

Snippets

So Morey died.

But in the best of ways.

Suddenly, from a heart attack.

Speaking of timing, good timing that was.

Less than 7 minutes with little to suffer.

Hardly time to see a patient.

Really kind of a silent attack with some shortness of breath.

But consider how death comes to many.

The bump was gone because there was no bump.

The tears were not there because no one saw them.

You don't need tears to know you are sad,

But they tell the world.

There was a time when I saw patients by looking at them.

They told me why they were there.

They didn't have to bring a bump.

They didn't have to bring anything.

We could talk about anything.

Even things you couldn't code.

Even things you couldn't see.

Even things you couldn't hear, taste, smell or touch.

I wonder what,

What was in her heart under the chest with no bump

I wonder what,

What my best instructor in medical school, Dr. Ward, would have said about my physical exam?

I wonder what,

What I did all that work for to become a doctor.

My son never went to a college football game.

Best time to study when the halls were quiet.

He's a doctor.

I never took a summer off from school from kindergarten on.

Best time to get ahead of others.

After high school graduation,

I drove from place to place, looking for friends.

Found none. No graduation party invitations.

But I had aced the philosophy test that morning.

Morey died about 3 months ago.

It was shortly after Ms. Gravitus had made the appointment.

The appointment to see me,

To get some help.

The appointment was made on the computer.

It will save all of medicine.

The government is requiring it.

It changes time.

The Cheyenne say, "Our first teacher is our own heart."

Ms. Gravitos should have spoken up.

She should have told me, "I'm over here.

Over here by the window.

Over here in the light of your God.

Over here in the place you asked me to be

Over here to talk to you, to tell you…

over here."

To Make Good Luck

My sister, actually my sister-in-law,

My wife, and myself

We are the makeshift

Crew of three.

We have been on a cruise together.

Love each others company.

Today we will go to the WWI museum.

It is magnificent.

Why in KC?

When trains were king,

The troops stopped by the thousands in Union Station

So that is the natural place for the best museum I will ever see.

Luck by definition is something you can't make.

Supposedly random.

Supposedly not by our own doing.

But today, a hot summer Saturday in July, I will politely disagree.

This is a great statement of faith on your part

And on my part.

Because seldom, if ever, do I politely disagree.

Disagreement, common; politely, uncommon.

So we will see how this goes.

It went not well in WWI.

A holocaust all its own

Which set us up for WWII and the real Holocaust.

So when Constance sees the museum,

She will see through the eyes that will cry.

Through eyes that will not judge.

Through intelligent eyes that will find solace in grief.

Here is where luck comes in.

It will appear lucky that she will find so much of faith.

Faith through carnage, through abject loss, through loss of life; all in one museum,

But it is not.

Constance makes her own luck:

Marriage of strife, cancer, single, sister slain

But she is a grandmother of royal qualities and may be the luckiest person I know.

Not sure of this luck origination, I am not sure she knows.

Doctors, like me,

Painfully aware of luck's importance,

I attempt to create it,

But I pale in comparison to Constance.

A friend's recent obituary in the paper this week.

It said, "No funeral, just remember me when you read a good book or take a fun trip."

Constance thought this quite good.

She wants a celebration of life.

She is a celebration of life.

Can be ebullient.

Can be a calm, positive force.

A laugh for the ages, eyes sparkling like no other.

At the beginning of the Museum,

There is an attempt to explain why there was war.

"A cleansing war would be good," an expert of the time explains.

So we cleansed: Jews in Germany, Armenians in Ottoman Empire, Bosnian Muslims in Bosnia, and American Indians in America.

So Constance would be a possible cleansing victim or survivor.

Not giving in if victim, not giving out if survivor.

How could someone of low dominion, like me, know this.

I could keep it a secret but I guess I won't.

She is of the race of humans

That can stand a fall but be of good faith,

Live or die with dignity,

Not trite.

So after we go to the museum,

I already know what she will say,

"Mercy, how mean we are to each other.

But there were good people too."

So she'll make a little hope.

Live with a little luck.

Luck she made a long time ago.

Saving My Life

I want to be Rip Van Winkle.

I think of it often.

But instead of sleep,

I'll just get in my car and drive in a straight line out West and disappear.

Everything will change without me.

That's what is scary.

Things won't be the same if I ever comeback.

And I will know nobody.

Mrs. DeJesus saved my life.

Snippets

She gave me the paper statues that stand on my office bookcase.

She bought them in Mexico.

They made her think of my wife and me.

I don't know her immigration story.

If her mother came here to have a baby so she could be an American?

If she was illegal and had a fake social security card?

If she might have been smuggled in like a butchered bovine?

We don't ask questions if the patient offers no answers.

That is how I see patients at the Free Health Clinic.

They are just patients.

I am just a doctor.

I have no training on immigration.

All I know about a green card is that it is green.

On some occasions in the clinic,

I feel just adequate to do my job to treat skin disease.

I will at least stay with something I know something about.

She sees me in my office now.

"I have a job and insurance and I can see you here now.

My rash is gone,

But it is not fair to take your time on the phone."

"You have a question?"

"My sister is mentally retarded and she has come from Mexico to live with me.

She is basically alright but has nightmares and must sleep with me.

I know this is not right. We are grown women."

"Who says it is not right?"

"The doctor, he says they will take her away from me if they find out."

I have never been able to fathom how someone could have mixed up Mrs. DeJesus.

So mixed up she was crazy.

"You are losing it. No one will or could enforce that,

It makes no sense."

"You who are a doctor and an American man,

You know nothing.

You do not know what they could do."

"Who told you this?

It is insane.

Do not go to that doctor again.

Are you making this up?"

"You say then it is OK?

It is not sinful?"

"Of course it is OK.

If it calms her,

It is the best of all things to do."

"So if I have other questions,

Will you be here?

You're not going anywhere?

I heard you were leaving."

"Who told you that?"

"I know you Dr. Hall.

I know you want to get away.

Is this not true?"

I have only seen Mrs. DeJesus three times in my life.

Twice at the free health clinic and now once in my office.

I regard her sanity as questionable at this point

And mine is in some question also.

"I will be here."

And I am here.

That was twenty years ago.

Mrs. DeJesus has never returned.

Snippets

She has disappeared.

But somehow I fear taking down the paper mache couple that peers at me from the wooden shelf.

The woman holds a washboard.

The man holds a pig.

They are dressed in gray polka dots.

That is how the discarded wrapping paper they are made of is decorated.

The man's hat is a piece of the stock market section of a newspaper.

The women's shoes appear to be the bottom of the cartoon section.

They are too realistic to be made of paper.

They are too smart to be standing mute.

They are firmly glued to their wooden blocks.

Their paper mouths in a straight line forever.

So I never got in my car.

I never drove away.

I am still waiting for Mrs. DeJesus.

I would run from everything for nothing.

She would run from nothing for everything.

You decide what is everything.

Snippets

Just like the couple made of paper.

God is watching.

I imagine Mrs. DeJesus wandering through a market.

Dragging along her sister.

They spot the paper couple.

Made from the trash of the street.

I also imagine her being deported,

With tears from friends and family.

Her sister being torn from her bed.

You can have a neighbor worse than Mrs. DeJusus.

Did they take her away?

Was my advice the reason?

You can have a neighbor worse than Mrs. DeJusus.

After all, she saved my life.

Forgiveness

We put people back together again.

We give them a new kidney,

A new liver, heart, lung.

Maybe a new attitude.

"Dear Dr. Hall.",

The heading of the scribbled note said.

It was on blue lined note paper that had been torn from its ringed moorings.

The page was a little wrinkled,

But all was legible.

"I saw the oncologist today and we agreed to sort of let things go.

I have started on hospice today and I thought you would like to know.

Thank you for all your kindnesses.

Yours truly, Mabel Gold."

So I like to procrastinate like everyone else,

But you can't procrastinate too long with someone on hospice.

The time had come for the phone call.

The call to Mabel Gold.

Mabel and I had been seeing each other for twenty years.

She was now 65 years old and a renal transplant patient.

Here is the amazing fact.

Her first transplant was when she was 25.

The first successful transplant was in 1954 in identical twins.

Snippets

The science has improved since.

But 40 years is an amazing longevity.

For a prim little lady from Carthage, Missouri.

She didn't need a new heart or liver or lung or attitude.

She just needed to borrow a filter.

To filter her blood,

To eliminate waste.

Someday we will just grow a new kidney from a cell in your skin.

It will be accepted gladly by your body's immune army.

But we won't do it today.

We might do it in time for your great grandchildren.

But probably not for you or Mabel Gold.

So to keep your part of choice,

We need to shut off your immune system.

Since it isn't really your part,

You borrowed it.

There are little devil cells in all of us.

They constantly are killed by our immune system.

But if we can't keep them on their silent inevitable death march

When the immune system is suppressed.

They live and kill us and we call them cancer.

Hence the great conundrum.

Balance saving your new part.

Or losing all your parts,

Due to the emperor of maladies.

Balance your diet.

Balance your balance.

Balance your checkbook.

But above all balance your immunity.

More people live with broken immunity.

More people get cancer.

More people die a slow agonizing death.

More people go on hospice.

More people die of cancer.

All because parts is parts.

You need your parts.

There are extra parts.

So you get new parts to keep going

or you don't keep going.

But Mabel would keep going.

She was invincible.

Her only cancer was squamous cell skin cancer.

It seldom is fatal.

The problem with seldom is:

It is not never,

It is not ever,

It is sometimes.

Sometimes is 100% if it's you

So it was with Mabel Gold.

Her cancer was in her lymph nodes that I felt one day.

Then her liver, Than her lungs, Then her brain.

Too many parts.

I use the phone too much.

I don't see people often enough.

I am too lazy.

I try to make it up with being benevolent.

So here goes benevolent.

"Mabel, I am truly sorry.

Is there anything to do? Another opinion?"

Snippets

"I don't think so,

We fought hard didn't we Dr. Hall?

The tumors just kept coming."

"They did and you did and I am truly sorry."

"It's for the best, Dr. Hall,

Thanks for calling."

Inadequate.

Lazy.

I missed one.

I used the phone too much.

I didn't see her often enough.

I didn't treat her aggressively enough.

I should have used the surgeons more.

I should have biopsied more.

I should have done something different.

I didn't tell her this.

I was afraid.

I was without excuse.

Only God can forgive some things.

Snippets

You can only forgive yourself so much,

So I won't forgive.

Mabel Sterling forgave.

But I did not.

God was silent.

There were no other opinions.

When I hung up the phone,

No other voice.

But then I thought I heard her again.

Mabel Gold.

"We gave it a good fight didn't we, Dr. Hall?"

That is all.

That is all.

That is all.

But is wasn't all.

You heard what Mabel said the second time, didn't you?

That was the benediction

As long as you heard it.

Then you give me my forgiveness.

Sometimes it must come from others.

So we can have it.

So we ourselves can have forgiveness.

Patches

There are patches in my garden where nothing grows.

It reminds me the earth is not mine and I can't claim it as mine.

The squirrels in my garden know this.

So they share it with me and bury their treasures to claim in spring.

The Kamba of Africa, the Lakota of America,

They know it too,

They believe it still.

They leave their ancestors there for the earth to claim.

The patches in my life that I can't seem to manage,

Where nothing grows.

They aren't mine to own either.

They are shared with others.

Mainly, Charlotte, my wife.

She never fails.

She fills in the patches with her precious thoughts for her God to claim.

All those empty places that no one can own.

They just wait and wait and wait

In winter the squirrels don't give up their patch of shared land.

Neither does Charlotte.

There is no way to care more than she does.

The Lakota and Kamba care too.

You say someone has to care?

But they don't have to.

They do it from love of the earth.

From their family.

From their friends.

Sometimes they do it for their God.

There are no graveyards for the Kamba or Lakota

They have no need to make the ground a holy place.

The earth is hallowed already.

Their faith made it so.

It would be a shame without those unconquered places.

Snippets

We only rent, we never own.

We only patch things up.

We never make them more perfect than they were before.

There is a patch in our hearts that is wild always.

The squirrels know all about it.

The Kamba and Lakota, they know.

Charlotte knows too.

God told them a long time ago and they never forgot.

Inside

Friday morning about 11:00 am at the free health clinic, Room # 3,

The air conditioning wasn't working that well.

The morning sun shown white hot through the window.

"What can I do for you?"

I have to stop here.

Stopping is what this is about.

That and the weather.

Do we need air conditioning?

So what would be the weather within those four walls?

Sweltering so you could smell the sweat between Mrs. Hutchins and I?

What about bringing in some wind if those four stained walls were swept away?

And a little rain right inside that room sending a message from our God?

Burning rays of sun shining between the spate of dark clouds?

Then the air conditioning clunked to a stop.

Then everything just stopped.

Then Mrs. Hutchins had stopped talking.

I was out of bright ideas.

Our visit should have been over.

Then the doorknob simply fell off the hollow wooden door as I tried to turn it and leave.

Locked inside.

Not an exit to be found.

So I sat back down and Mrs. Hutchins did the silent shaking laugh that only those of significant girth can really do right.

And it was quiet and I remember that everything stopped.

We looked at each other inside that room.

We were so far away.

Black and white.

Poor and rich.

Fat and thin.

Alone and lonely.

Suddenly, we were the same.

The space between us had a name just like us.

If you named that space then it didn't seem so vast.

So we each sat on our side of the space but connected.

Still. Stopped.

The day had just gone away and it was without the weather.

Would we be trapped in there forever?

Was it to be endless morning?

Here is where it just gets strange.

We didn't call for help.

We didn't bang on the door.

We didn't stand on a chair and peek over the transom to see who was there.

We stopped still.

Now we were really the same.

We wanted to sit and rest there a little bit longer.

Without the rain and wind and sun of ourselves.

Without the torrents and hurricanes of life.

"There is always the weather to talk about in the Midwest," my mother would say.

It is always newsy and always changes.

It changes how the farmers' lives turn out.

It changes how you feel on Sunday afternoons.

I don't know how long we were there.

Maybe I'm still in there.

Something holy is.

Just Mrs. Hutchins and me.

Weather Forecast Inside Room: 333, 11:55 am

Conditions: Fair, Stuffy

Wind: None in any direction

Barometric Pressure: Steady, Unchanged

Humidity: 73%

Forecast: Very Still

Extended Forecast: Still

Still inside.

February

It's February.

The dreary, gray month that we survive only because of Valentine's Day and Mardi Gras.

And I'm just in the middle of it.

Ruth Klausen is 87,

She can't stop scratching.

She can't stop itching.

"Where?" I say.

" Now it's on the back of my neck."

"It says on your chart that oncology increased your pills."

"They didn't."

"Let me see your neck.

It's the lymphoma in the skin that is flaring and making you itch."

A large tear rolls down her right cheek and splashes onto her white blouse.

Her head tips to the right due to her humpback that tilts that way.

She is way too thin but that is not new.

The wisp of hair hanging over her forehead is so white it lights the room.

Square framed black glasses hide the biggest brown eyes I will see this month.

Her face is small, round, and soft with just a few crinkles over her prominent tiny cheeks.

Her lips are pale and her mouth seems invisible.

She has one living relative.

It is her husband for whom she cares for with the "A" disease.

We never talk about it much.

"You're depressed?"

"I don't want more pills."

"Do you have a church?"

"Ascension."

"I can call them to see if someone could visit."

"I haven't been there in two years."

"We will increase your chemo and add an anti-itch lotion."

"I will see you in 6 weeks and not 3 months to see how your are doing."

"It really is the sign that makes me cry".

"The sign?"

"It's on the wall over the mirror."

"And what does it say"

'If You Can Think It ,Then You Can Do It.'

And I do, I think it every day.

But I still can't stop the itch.

I've never told anyone that before."

I freeze a spot on her neck.

"That might help."

It is my last patient before lunch and I'm tired.

I am getting up to hurry out.

After all, I am a busy physician in the age of digital corporate medicine.

Time is money.

But I work for myself so when she says,

"Come back and sit down."

I do just that.

"Thanks for everything so much," she says.

"For what?'

"For listening about the sign."

"Sure."

I already know what I will do in 6 weeks.

I will increase the medicine again because she won't be better yet.

I'll see if some neighbor or someone from my church can look in on her.

But only if she'll let me.

I feel like saying, "take down the sign" but I don't.

I feel like saying, "you will get better" but I don't.

I feel like saying," just keep thinking what the sign says and you will get

better" but I don't.

I just give her a quiet, loose hug.

We don't talk again that day.

Really, why should we?

After all, it's February.

The gray, dreary month.

It's the shortest month of the year you know.

Saint Valentine may have been a minister to martyrs.

On the 15th day the Romans had a festival of purification.

I'm in the middle of it.

I'm just in the middle of it.

Monarchs

The monarch butterfly

On the brink of extinction

So I built a butterfly garden

Let the asclepias sing.

Roberto Sivilas isn't a dwarf.

But he is close.

He is not the least handsome of my cadre of patients.

But he is close.

Sometimes in the science of medicine

Kidneys shut down.

We used to read the last rites.

You need to be with kidney,

To be with life.

Now we use dialysis.

Beats death.

But Dialysis changes people.

Lethargic, amotivational, and depressed.

Roberto didn't start out in a funky dialysis sort of way,

He had great hopes of finding a kidney.

But God gave him a little quirk.

His genetic makeup was a tricky match.

Genetic matches are less important for transplants now.

But they weren't then.

On the transplant list for 20 years.

"How is it going Roberto?"

"I've given up.

NO matches and I can't take it.

Dialysis forever.

I can't take the waiting."

So don't think God doesn't like statistics:

Chance, mathematics, odds, roll of the dice.

Roberto was tired of rolling the immune markers.

Came up craps every time.

So the Monarch butterfly,

The brain smaller than a grain of sand.

Yet three generations from Canada to Mexico remember.

They remember where they go to winter.

But the winter habitat is fading.

Habits are hard to break.

So the Monarch must change its choice of winter vacation.

Or perish.

You can't usually do dialysis forever,:

Infections, access site depletion, suicide.

So my first cousin became exhausted from dialysis.

Snippets

So she quit and left her husband of 56 years.

"You seem chipper today, Roberto."

"Got married."

"Fantastic!"

"She wants to run her markers to see if she can donate a kidney."

"Great, Do it!"

"No, it would be the final disappointment."

"She wants to do it, let her."

"Stay out of this Doc."

So the monarch butterfly survives on only one plant.

It is the milkweed.

Eats on it, breeds on it, and survives only on it,

Can't live without it.

Last summer, I found a monarch caterpillar,

And put it in a jar for the grandkids.

It made a chrysalis on the underside of lid.

Became a butterfly overnight.

I put it back in the milkweed patch.

The patch carefully grown in my backyard.

Told it goodbye.

Never saw it again.

Saw Roberto one last time as well.

His skin disease had resolved.

It was dialysis induced.

Not on dialysis anymore.

"My wife was a perfect match.

Thanks for everything Doc.

I'm in a hurry.

You know the routine, honey-do's."

So here is the deal.

God had made a bet one last time for Roberto.

She won.

Snippets

Roberto won.

I bet on one last monarch.

The butterfly and its progeny probably will disappear forever.

The odds are not in its favor.

For the Pima Indians, it is a harbinger of winter.

My daughter, Shelly, sent me a Father's day card last year.

Covered with Monarchs.

"Love, it means more than you will ever know,"

Is written on the cover.

I want to believe the Monarchs will make it.

The Nahauati people of Mexico,

They say the Monarchs are the souls of the dead.

Surely our souls will live forever.

Playing the game of chance again,

God's luck will decide the end game.

But She is on a roll,

Just ask Roberto Sivilas.

Peonies

The plants that last forever are the peonies.

Found in English gardens a century old,

All the garden awash in weeds, but the peonies still grow and bloom.

They will never flower unless they live through a winter frozen.

The peonies that grew in my father-in-law's garden,

They grew in his mother's garden before.

When he died we dug them up and gave them to my sister who is a master gardener, my nephew, a patient, and myself to plant in the backyard.

We are quite the novices.

The Chinese perfected this flower over 3,000 years

Dividing tubers, harvesting seed.

All the right things to perfect the perfect flower.

Moorfield Gardens is a famous flower farm in Northern Ireland.

Even though it seems peonies like growing in Ireland,

Only recently have they been added to their repertoire.

Strange to skip an island for so many centuries.

The world of people had never seen this, before or after.

One fourth of a country, Ireland, starved to death in a single generation.

They called it "the famine generation" from 1845 to 1870.

2.5 million fled to America.

My ancestors, the British,

Could somehow be so cruel.

1871 to 1921 another 2.1 million came to land founded by British Colonists.

In America, again, they could somehow be so cruel.

Isek Denison took peonies to Kenya.

She thought they would not bloom because she picked too early.

Not so.

Barren of flowers they were, as no freeze there was.

Snippets

They love peonies in Hawaii.

But they would never bloom.

Until they threw ice on them in the winter.

They needed icy cold to bud.

Charlotte is my wife.

Her grandfather came to Jasper, Nebraska

His father was Irish to the core.

Grandpa lost everything in the depression.

Even lost his mind.

He spent 22 years in a Mental Institute.

An alcoholic.

All blamed on being Irish.

In the brown eyes of Charlotte,

I saw bloom but did not know it was from the Isle.

I saw the peonies come late to her homeland where they are called
peony roses.

Her parents now dead had kept the secret of Irish blood.

Snippets

My lover found where her grandfather's father was born forever Irish.

My daughter lived in France with a secret wish of being from the "Irish".

The red-haired pixie had friends attach a name.

They called her Irish.

She danced a bit of a mental jig.

When she heard the news.

I knew something was hidden before the facts appeared.

Just like peonies late to the island, I found the missing link late in Charlotte's eyes.

It was Ireland all along.

The bitter cold, the suffering, but survival had to happen.

To see the bloom of the Irish peonies,

In Charlotte's rosy cheeks.

It was worth it.

All the loss leaves all the gain.

All the leaving, just the pain.

Before the glory.

Snippets

Ireland will live with me forever.

Maybe I could become Irish someday.

If they would let me in,

Forgive my English sins.

Alas, it will not happen.

But do not mourn for me.

I have the best a Brit could have.

The love from one of those we sought to destroy.

She is Ireland and she will last forever.

The Firing Squad

The firing squad.

Cheapest, most humane, most deadly, most noble.

Six shooters, one with blanks, so less guilt for gunners.

Aim for the heart.

Snippets

Organs available for harvest,

Body available for burial,

Corpse can be identified.

Last time done in USA, 1996.

I have heard there are some secrets that are best kept secret,

Like the names of people.

But I have been told by my wife, a member of a hefty throng,

That keeping secrets is not my forte.

So I have to give you his name,

I tried to write the story without it,

Williams, Duckworth, Smith, Morales?

But I am left with the real name, a secret no longer: Steelman.

There I have said it and I see him still.

Not fifty years ago,

Not a dream,

But standing here now looking over my shoulder.

All my medical career, I have admired surgeons the most.

Physical, mental, emotional stamina without end.

Could I have been one?

Never in a million stitches.

So I tried to write this with a surrogate moniker.

But the words were not there.

It had to be the old man of steel.

The man of Steelman.

The British call it the identity parade,

As potential perpetrators of a crime are lined up.

Only one is guilty,

The eyewitness picks that one, however inaccurate.

Gordy Winchek, medical student, was sort of a wingnut,

From a small town in Nebraska.

We are standing in the doctor's lounge, waiting for the aforementioned, Steelman.

"I have had it; we admit and do the paper work for Steelman's crocks.

Snippets

We get nothing for it.

Steelman gets our services for nothing.

Then we get to hold a retractor for 3 hours for nothing.

Nothing but history and physicals late into the night for nothing.

Steelman doesn't care."

Part of this rant may have truth.

But a more potent truth is this.

Steelman is standing there.

Fear of surgeons, especially thoracic and neurosurgeons.

This is a medical students recurring nightmare.

A nightmare no longer.

This is reality in all its horrible glory.

In the Saint Valentine's day massacre,

Bugs Moran's thugs of the Irish Mafia,

Murdered by Al Capone's thugs of the Italian Mafia,

And Capone thought he had killed Moran.

Snippets

There is now silence.

Not of the white-coated lambs but the white-coated medical students.

The silence of the line up,

The silence before the firing squad fires.

"Please line up against the wall, gentlemen."

Five altogether and one was me.

I suspected Steelman was not with weapon.

But Steelman was with Steelman.

Flashback, two weeks before.

First night for medical student Hall in ER.

Young male athlete with acute abdomen.

Bleeding to death from ruptured spleen.

Steelman on call and appears from nowhere.

Coattails flying.

"Get my instruments!

Clean this belly!"

Snippets

He opened him up in the hallway.

Nothing but blood everywhere.

"Who is holding that retractor?

I can't see a thing."

So amidst the chaos was a high squeaking noise echoing off the ceiling.

My shoes sliding across the recently buffed linoleum floor.

Muscles strained pulling back the ribcage of the man with the torn spleen.

Losing the battle but no one else to do the job.

"That's why girls don't go into surgery, Hall."

How he had time to insult me with everything going on I will never know.

"Got the artery! The bleeding should stop."

Like the finger in the dike the spurt of fluid abruptly halted.

So I had reason to fear the Steelman.

Six men in a room and only one with bullets.

And he shot straight through the five of hearts.

"Listen well, those who want to be doctors."

There are many bad doctors,

But there are no bad patients.

You can learn from every patient.

Write down what you learn from each of my patients."

He never checked if we did but we certainly did,

I remember his voice as clear as the stalactites of ice that hang from my roof.

I think of it often when a patient seems too routine,

Too mundane, too unworthy of my attention.

"Many bad doctors, but no bad patients."

I spent most waking hours for the next month holding a retractor for Steelman.

Less exciting cases but never routine.

He did no routine cases.

"Here again Hall, what are you doing here?"

End of the month.

"I'll give you a recommendation if you ever need it, Hall."

I never asked him.

I felt somehow unworthy.

But sometimes I wished I had asked him.

Just to show I could do it.

Just to pretend I deserved it.

Even if I knew I never would.

Never worthy enough to be in front of the firing squad.

You Can Do What You Want to Do?

I could only write this using the patient's real name.

I went back and changed it later.

I've thought of whom I've lost later.

And later that's what I can still see very clearly as if it was today.

Charles Randall Langworthy.

Of the famous Langworthy's.

Who built the two biggest financial empires in the city.

Snippets

A family most momentous and generous.

Charles was the most amazing.

Saved a monument to a president.

Saved a symphony.

Saved one of the nations greatest engineering firms.

Gave me a list one day.

"This is a private list.", John.

It will save your free health clinic.

Use my name as the seed donor and it will be done.

So my favorite place to work is where I work for free.

So I volunteer.

And I work my little tail off.

It is third world medicine in a first world country.

The care is good.

But the resources poor.

Am I in Kenya, Haiti, South Sudan, the slums of Rio?

No, the land of the free.

Can you be with the shackles of poverty, free?

Can you be with the worry of no food?

No medical care, no place of affordable education?

No transportation, no network?

So the clinic survives today because of Langworthy.

He wants no credit.

He just came in for a last visit he was keenly aware that he didn't really need.

He tells me today his colon cancer is metastatic to the liver.

An all too common malady.

Charles Langworthy, President Regan, and one of my best friends,

Did not get regular colonoscopies.

Killed my friend, almost killed a President, and now will kill Charles Randle Langworthy.

The watery salty tears did not mix well with the fabric of his silk suit.

The shoulder was the strongest.

The hug the best.

The words the purest, "you are a good man, John."

I really did not want to be a good man.

I just wanted Charles Langworthy to live a little longer.

Who knows what he might save next.

Maybe the world at the precipice.

He could go wherever he wanted to go,

And he could do whatever he wanted to do.

But just one last time.

He wasn't in the business of self-pity.

So he said in a matter of fact voice.

"I have traveled the world but never seen the Oregon coast.

They say it is rugged beyond beautiful.

That is where I will go."

So today I am thanking Charles.

For all he kept from harm.

Snippets

I can see him in the salt spray,

Overlooking the Pacific.

He could have started in Astoria and taken highway 101 south.

I did that when I was 10 years old but don't remember it.

I should have gone with him like his memory has gone with me.

We could have talked of the worries of the world.

Here is the truth:

He could do whatever he wanted to do.

He had no commitment for the last weeks.

But death limits your options or makes them limitless.

Like all of us,

Charles Randall Langworthy had made some friends and made some enemies.

But he left more than he took.

That is all heroes have to do.

If I ever see him again,

I will tell him about this hero stuff.

The stuff he never thought he was.

The stuff he most certainly looked more like than most.

Right now, his memory is more than I will ever deserve.

For Kate

Kate is my niece.

My older sister's youngest child.

She is the perfect niece.

She's beautiful, of course.

She saves people.

She saved her mother from cancer.

She saved marine biology.

She saved Belize.

Katie is a young lady.

I am an old man.

But Katie and I have a few things in common.

We both live in America.

Snippets

You know America.

The United States of America.

The country made up by the British.

I've saved a few things of my own.

I saved medicine

I tried to save my mother from depression

I saved Kenya.

So Kenya and Belize were also made up by the British

Who left them two of the poorest countries of the world.

No one could save them from poverty.

But Kate and I saved them from everything.

So after we saved these countries,

We realized we weren't saving America

America, land of the free, the brave, and the noise.

After we saved those countries we had to learn to love the noise again.

It's kind of hard to reappear in the land of the rich.

We could get lost in those other places.

Snippets

No one knew who we were.

Responsibilities weren't overwhelming.

When you save those ravaged, by having nothing, it isn't that hard.

They, of course, are happy.

We, of course, in America can't decide if we are happy.

We don't know what happiness is.

We are constantly making the noise in pursuit.

When it gets quiet in America, which isn't often, then we are in Kenya and Belize again.

I dream of Kate and I standing on the sands of Belize or the highlands of Kenya.

We are brave then, standing in a slight breeze of danger, the people love us.

We love the people.

It is quiet.

It is just liberating.

We have learned to love the noise again, Kate probably better.

But Kate and Belize, and I and Kenya are somehow bound together.

We have seen those who are happy and quiet who have nothing.

We, of course, have everything.

Snippets

You know, America has everything.

And America will find out what happiness is.

It just takes some countries longer than others.

And by the way, we haven't saved America yet.

When we do, we will put it some place safe.

Next to Kenya and Belize.

Yet, I should add that it's going to be hard, of course.

Complaining on Father's Day 2015

We complain often.

We complain about the weather.

We complain about our parents, siblings, and children.

We complain about work and vacations.

We all complained through history.

We did it at the Holocaust.

We did it at Nuremberg.

We did it at Selma.

We did it at the Civil War.

We did it at Andersonville where my great uncle's life was ruined forever.

At Pearl Harbor, in the Philippines, at Hiroshima.

We complained about Pilate, and Hitler, Isis, and Abu Ghraib.

We have new complaints about the fate of the most migrants ever.

They have no country, no food, no water, and maybe no hope.

My father said complaining was a bad habit.

And I know what he meant.

But now we have Charleston, Sandy Hook, Orlando, Dallas.

We are complaining again.

God is not complaining,

He is drying the tears and healing the souls.

We are not God.

We are still complaining.

I will complain forever.

I hope my father hears me.

I hope your father hears you.

I hope fathers are listening everywhere,

My father, your father, their fathers, our Father.

Three O'clock in the Morning

"Who do you call?" my minister said, and where are you

At three O'clock in the morning?

There is a place to go and be forever.

It feels safe there and separate.

The physics gurus say the black space is full of energy.

I agree, I can feel it.

So my minister asks, "who do you call?

Who do you call if you need some peace?

My father always woke at 3:00 AM

Accurate as a clock.

His shingles pain never let him forget the time.

For seven long years and then he died.

The same wake-up time for Mrs. Teal,

Who helps care for her husband on hospice.

Teal, the color of the Intercessors of the Lamb,

Who symbolize the community between heaven (blue) and earth (green).

Same time for my daughter with terminal insomnia to start to stir.

Same time for thunder to salute for all to wake up.

Same time for my panic attacks.

It is indeed the time my watch currently reads.

Purgatory, it may not be so bad,

If you sit like a tri-cornered stone in the dust,

On the road to the Cathedral in Victoria, Kansas,

You may well be picked up by a deity as a keepsake.

Those people of the dust bowl.

They knew 3:00 in the morning.

They knew you have to see faith.

When you can't see anything.

It is beyond the present and in the black space.

How I love the black and dark spaces in the night.

You can see endlessness.

You can feel the seeping away of mindlessness.

There is someone there who talks so quiet.

So quiet that the peace is not disturbed.

The music is so intense that you can't hear it.

That is who you call.

The best friend that you always wanted but never had.

He will listen,

Reassure you,

Capture your heart and your meaning.

You can only be with him in the night.

He doesn't curse the darkness.

He doesn't ask questions.

He doesn't have to speak.

Snippets

He is just your friend.

The friend you always had but never knew it.

The person who you call at three O'clock in the morning.

He lives in the place you always said you would go but never went.

But you can be there now.

No criticism from others.

No noise from the outside.

Just drift away.

Into the dark, quiet, peaceful, empty void of where you know

You were always meant to be.

But could never get there.

At least you thought could never get there.

But you can get there now.

Humming

You know this story is not about humming.

There is a man in our church,

Let's call him Albert.

Elder, usher, cleans the sanctuary.

He constantly whistles.

Albert whistles off tune and out of rhythm with no discernable pattern.

A friend of mine in choir

Approached Albert one day.

"Can't you carry a tune,

Perhaps try a real song?"

This was not a compliment but fazed Albert not in the least.

For some unknown reason,

I have started humming in church.

I am never far off on note or beat,

But I would like to be right on.

My father always thought I was a great singer.

My great talent was supposedly from said father who actually was a great singer,

But I knew better.

My minister thought not of my singing,

And still knows not of it now.

Our new and current minister gives great sermons.

I saw my chance to prove my father right.

Sat in the front row, loud to all around,

So my great skills could be heard.

I knew the new man of the cloth would soon ask for me to join the choir.

Alas, there was not summons nor questions about my talents.

My wife,

Snippets

Always kind,

Was curious about my robust voice,

But silent.

This was the one and only front row performance.

Today my eldest attended church with me and wife.

She can sing, inherited from her mother's father.

I could not reach the hymnal quite it time,

So I began to hum.

You can hide a lot with a hum and still enjoy the music.

My high school choir teacher,

"Someone is off in the baritone section."

I mouthed the words,

"Now you've got it."

You can only deceive the sounds of the angels for so long.

But here is the thing:

Moved him, and befriended a caregiver and life was better.

Caregivers in nursing homes:

Love work

Underpaid

Overworked

In 2012, 212 Billion Dollars in USA for long term elderly care.

By 1920, 5 million over 65.

By 2060, 92 million over 65.

11% of patients over 85 in nursing homes in USA today.

In 2012, 1.3 million people lived in nursing homes USA.

Tired of numbers.

Saw Tan today, from Vietnam.

Married and lives with mother and plans to care for her when she is elderly.

In the religion of the people who first occupied where I live,

The great chief, Black Elk,

He believed that the entire universe was a series of hoops,

With the family as the center circle.

In the religion I claim to believe,

The family is at the center.

You took care of family,

Abandonment was not an option.

Cambodia, Vietnam, Lakota Nation, early Christianity, not a lot of nursing homes.

Approximately 15,400 certified nursing homes in USA,

Both my grandmothers had their daughters live with them till the end. (One daughter, severe invalid).

My daughter and my only 2 grandchildren live with my wife and I.

Father-in –law,

Raised on a farm in the depression.

Almost killed by a drug the doctor forgot he prescribed.

Always thought dogs should remain outside.

He lived on the couch in our den for 4 weeks.

The best 4 weeks of my 3 children's lives and the inside dog.

Snippets

Dad was wisdom, and love.

Friend to the dog.

Respect for the elderly,

Might be missing,

Could be found,

But have to seek it out, they don't want to bother you.

"Does your mother live in a nursing home?" I asked.

Kalliyan was coming off a long day of work.

She had seen the haze of the dog days of summer.

They were barking at her right now.

"Tell Doctor Hall that he will not see my mother today.

She lives with me.

Enough insults for this week.

We are leaving,

In our culture we know our family is life and we are living."

I threw myself on the threshold of the God of Mercy.

"Tell her I am sorry.

I am ignorant.

I am disrespectful."

There is a river I have dreamed of living by with the grandfather minister I never knew.

We could hear the rush of the water at night.

We could wade in the cold water in the day.

We would get hot in the day, but we were always cool at night.

That river is where I wanted to be the day I met Killiyan.

I admired her.

I admired her culture.

I suddenly felt sorry for America.

The Temple was razed,

But the people saved their God in the family.

We razed the family,

May God have mercy on our souls.

Snippets

I did not feel sorry for Killiyan, (means "of superior quality") she had plenty on her "to-do" list.

She had to pick up her kids from school.

There was grocery shopping to do,

And she had to find her mother another dermatologist.

The ageless aged keep quiet in their minds

The sounds they make are just a façade.

They are garbled to the outside world.

Inside their brains the world is seen going by.

"You judge me not by the outside," they say,

But read behind my eyes

I am here and see you.

Stay awhile if you can.

All that wisdom and love packed in stacks of buildings.

Get your bucket list and do it.

Get your piece of the pie.

Don't let those of age slow you down.

If you do, then you could get bogged down:

In Love.

In Wisdom.

In the great soul of the old.

You might even become a friend to the dog.

In the Beginning

Coldplay(rock group) said it best,

"I'm going back to the start."

To the beginning.

In the beginning:

There was a woman, a man, and a child who were sick.

Someone called them patients.

They saw someone to make them better.

Let's call them a physician.

"Patient" old French from latin for "suffering".

"Physician" old French from latin "for things related to nature."

The Egyptian, Imhotep, was the first physican known by name.

"Diagnostic Handbook" of etiology and therapy done in ancient Babylon.

Aescelapius, Hippocrates, Hutchinson, Pasteur, Harvey, Cushing.

Notice, no mention of payment.

Jesus, Buddha, Mother Theresa: All the best of physicians.

Notice, no mention of payment.

Hippocratic oath

Revised many times

"First do no harm."

Notice, no mention of payment.

I am a hopeless believer in charity.

I know, all charity, no capitalism.

No Donald Trump.

No Empire State Building.

 No war.

No competition.

No being #1.

No real fun.

But I can't help it.

The soaring prices of medicines in this country is ruining medicine,

And I want to give my patients the best drug available.

Regardless of price.

I really shouldn't be a doctor in America.

I really shouldn't be a doctor.

I just want to take care of people.

But I confess only 10% of my care is given for free.

Hypocrite and not Hippocrates is my life,

Free medical care—won't work, I know that.

But this isn't working.

We now have medical care for the rich of the world.

It might be if I lived back at the start.

A pharaoh, a king, a bishop, they could give me my living.

They could give me my status.

I could give them good medical care.

That's it,

"I'm going back to the start."

Hope my family and friends come.

Hope my church comes.

There should still be sunsets.

Sunrises were around even then.

We could have meetings and talk about medicine.

Think how much knowledge I could carry back.

My enormous ego would be satiated.

The king might give me time off.

More time off since he would be so grateful.

Medicine for everyone?—probably not.

They are just dreams of going back and medicine for free.

But it would at least be interesting,

So that's what I'm going to do today after I leave my office,

I'm going to do it for me.

"I'm going back to the start."

"I'm going back to the beginning."

Last Words

Walter Madison was not doing well.

Hard to pinpoint the exact cause of his malaise.

He was 98 and was in heart failure.

So we both realized this might be his last visit.

His son brought him in a wheelchair.

He was ashen and cachetic.

Snippets

We had been friends for the first 35 years of my practice.

I had known him also as a stalwart member of my church

"Just in to have a few spots looked at.

Feeling low recently,

So I wanted to thank you for your help

You know, in case I don't make it back."

So as my nurse and I eased him back into his wheelchair,

"Just wanted to say a few last words,

Don't know about the church these days,

Too friendly to gays, so see what you can do."

Last words.

I don't remember any last words.

From anybody, ever.

Now I was privy to these.

AIDS was evil.

It did unwanted things.

Even to those who did not have it.

It taught us who couldn't wait to revile homosexuality.

Jason Livey was a patient of mine.

Saw him at the free health clinic,

He was dying of AIDS,

This was at a time when AIDS and death were one word.

I thought of Jason.

On the day of the "last words."

He was a friend too,

In the kingdom of man.

Since the AIDS epidemic began 25 years earlier,

The Free Clinic had given care for free to 900 AIDS patients.

The largest AIDS group in our city,

A labor of love.

Hard to get a dermatologist to volunteer,

So a retired derm lady-angel and I,

We did all their skin care and

Wrote a book about it 19 years later.

AIDS in the Post HAART Era

Wrote it with my son, a skin pathologist.

A labor of love,

Could write a separate book about the writing of the book.

Not a best seller.

Sent a copy to George W.

To thank him for all the AIDS money he helped appropriate.

Someone sent back a nice note.

The book was just giving something back.

Something to thank all the AIDS patients.

For all they taught me.

For all they gave me.

Jason knew his pneumonia was fatal.

He knew this was his last hospitalization.

Snippets

He knew we were out of meds.

So his partner and I sat on the bed for a few minutes.

"Jason and I, sure as hell, will be glad,

Glad not to see the 'butcher of broadway,'

Meanest dermatologist on the planet.

Why are you so bloodthirsty?"

Three men, on a bed, in a hospital.

Then laughing and then crying.

For the life of me, or Jason, or his mate,

I don't remember any last words.

So my wife says,

"Walter could have said worse,

It just was a concern he had."

So tolerant she was tolerant of the intolerant.

So I am going to believe

That if Walter had spent 30 years with me,

Snippets

It might have taken much less,

He would have different words.

A secretary had changed her mind,

Completely changed after a year in my office.

She learned you have to observe another man's shoes,

To see how another man walks.

But I know this:

Jason died with dignity,

With as much goodness and love in his heart,

With as much of my heart, as anyone.

Gay patients bleed the same.

They live the same.

They die the same.

They cry the same.

The same as us.

You know, us.

Snippets

Human us.

All of us.

Walter's last words,

I will say them the way he would have,

If he had lived with me for 30 years,

When I was watching all those shoes.

Nowhere are gay people different,

Except in the way straight people treat them.

That is it,

The only difference.

So my wife has taught me many things,

Besides tolerance for all.

She has taught forgiveness,

Remember she is married to me.

So there is forgiveness

In life as in death.

Snippets

We all deserve another chance.

It is the way of God.

"It sure is great to see our church.

Open and welcoming.

As God would want it.

As I would want it."

What a great guy Walter could have been.

It would have been a great uplifting joy in my life forever.

To hear those "last words."

Rainout

Wearing a soft gray uniform

With magenta stripes down the sides no less.

Garish burnt orange hat with an italicized black L on the front.

And I was ready for my baseball game.

Snippets

The first and only year that I played organized baseball.

My parents never attended the games.

Which I only thought unusual years later.

It was OK, because at sports I was the worst.

It also occurred to me years later

Maybe my athletic prowess was poor

Because of no practice.

Since not friends, parents or siblings took the time.

In junior high and still taking piano lessons.

The lessons ended immediately before the game was to start

So I was to wait outside the teacher's house.

Thus my mother would pick me in the dirt steel-colored Plymouth.

Whisking me off just in time for the game.

Dropping me off at the field.

Not wishing me luck.

Which was just as well.

I still remember waiting for her in the driveway, of the piano teacher.

Who decides what times we will never forget?

The white enormous clouds with the black anvil base

Portended rain in Lincoln, Nebraska.

Let's get this straight from the beginning,

I love rain.

To make it the best rain ever,

If it started now the game might be rained out.

Yes! The "rainout" and it was the last game.

I could avoid the cat calls,

The groans and moans,

Baseballs deceiving me on purpose.

Baseball is king in Detroit, Michigan.

That was where I did my medicine internship.

Phone call from the chief of department,

He was the Tigers' team physician.

Snippets

He wanted me to admit Phil Hanson to the hospital.

Yes, the same Phil Hanson rookie for the Tigers.

He was to be the next Al Kaline

And I would get to meet him.

"Hey, my name is John Hall.

Here to do your admitting physical."

"No time now, I have to get on the plane.

Look how long the line is."

"You see a plane?"

"Over there by the window.

Boy what a day

And now I'm going to miss the plane."

"You had a great first game.

Sacrifice bunt, single, and a standing ovation.

Maybe a little too much excitement for first game.

I can see how that might happen."

Snippets

"Through the window.

I could jump through the window.

Wouldn't have to wait in line.

What do you think?"

Not a lot of meaningful facts here,

Except our baseball player had no facts.

Hallucinations galore but no facts.

"I think we can get someone to help you."

"Dr. Goodsend, your ballplayer is in far left field.

Hallucinating badly,

I think I can get a psyche consult tonight.

Rain the rest of the week so he may not miss that much ball."

No rainout for the rookie.

No rainout for me.

Brief baseball career for the rookie.

Brief baseball career for me.

Snippets

I, cut short by talent,

Rookie, cut short by illness,

But neither got help

From the rain.

Never saw the rookie again,

Just know what is on the internet.

Never really caught on in the bigs,

Maybe a mental thing but he loved that game.

I would have liked a hallucination or two

Could talk to my dad but he is not at my piano recital.

Not at my high school graduation, I was speaker.

Not at my medical school graduation, but I loved that guy.

My last game.

Bases loaded in the bottom of the ninth,

Coach gave the bunt sign.

Not much help since I was never told the bunt sign.

Struck out to end the game.

Coach went beserk.

Not hallucinating.

But acting crazy.

I only thought about this later.

But people don't usually hope for a rainout.

But don't sell the deluge short.

It can tell you a lot about life.

So rainouts can save you,

But not forever.

Here is the thing.

Long before our games, the rookie and I, we had already had a rainout.

I still love the rain.

The rookie, I'll never know, I hope, he too, still loves the rain.

Today

I have never written

About an event the day it happened.

It happened, in fact,

Sometime earlier today.

"Mrs. Wentzel,

Your skin looks great.

No need to see you again

For six months."

"Well I just have something I want to ask you before I leave.

Went to the GI doctor for my colonoscopy last year.

He said no problems and, at 83,

We were done with the scope exams.

So I had a pain in my right side last week.

They did another look with the colonoscope.

Grade IV colon cancer.

Snippets

It is in my liver.

They want to do chemotherapy.

I said no.

The doctors were not happy.

I trust you, what do you think?"

There is a saying I heard,

About trust and hope,

"you can hope to trust,

or trust to hope."

Not being the right person

At the right time

Is an occupational hazard

For any profession.

So today was just another day.

So I am depressed every morning,

Know I won't make it but I do.

Two different chemicals help.

Crazy, but Mrs. Wentzel has perked me up.

She trusts me and she knows,

I have no answers,

And I never will.

Ten billion planets that are in the correct locations,

Right distance from their stars,

Might have water.

Could have life.

"And that is just in our galaxy,"

Said the lady physicist on the radio.

"You can't believe there is no life elsewhere.

Not logical."

So I told my patient,

"There is an oncologist at the Med center,

He has been in the same place as you, great empathy.

I will get you an appointment if you wish."

"I am too old,

My children say don't do chemo.

Would you do chemo?"

"I don't know."

It seems I say "I don't know" more often these days.

As I age, so do my patients.

I'm feeling better sitting there with Mrs. Wentzel.

For no reason, I know, she is very grateful.

So when I heard about the abundance of planets today,

I wondered if I would ever see Mrs. Wentzel again.

I have a friend, a choir director in a church,

She is convinced in all the cosmos there is a circle.

She is convinced the molecules just get rearranged.

She in not a physicist.

She does not believe in an afterlife of self.

Just the molecules.

Mrs. Wenzel has a great smile.

I will always remember that smile.

I probably won't find out her decision.

Six months is a long time with grade IV colon cancer.

But we both felt better.

I got to see her great smile.

She got to talk to someone.

The molecules keep rolling around.

Maybe I'll bump into Mrs. Wentzel again.

I can't believe there is no life elsewhere.

I might get to thank Mrs. Wentzel.

But it's not logical.

If I were to see her again,

I would say I am sorry for all of this.

I would say I miss her for all of this.

I would say I love her for all of this.

What a day was today.

Did I tell you she had a great smile?

Locked

There was a plastic surgeon I once knew.

Long since deceased.

A story of him, however,

Lives with me forever.

Riley Simpson had a daughter,

The daughter's name, Caitland Riley Simpson.

They ended up calling her Riley Two.

It forever tied the mother and daughter.

They were one of those mother-daughter combos

That at times were more like sisters,

Snippets

And enjoyed each as much as friends,

As family.

So Riley Two was born with a 4 inch spot on her leg

When she was twelve it changed colors.

When I saw it my expression changed colors.

Melanoma at this age, almost unheard of, never seen it, but deadly.

So the Sun God said,

"I will give you life,

For wind, for rain, for food, for life itself."

And who would doubt the Sun God.

But as with all the Gods

The Sun God giveth and taketh away.

He takes away lives by causing the cancer I chase every working day.

The melanoma.

Dr. Lock was the best plastic surgeon I knew in Kansas City.

Especially good with children.

Snippets

I wanted the tumor removed but I also wanted the least scar possible.

Who would not choose Dr. Lock?

"No, sorry John, I can't accept insurance.

Cash only. I've given up on all insurance. They just don't pay enough."

"She could never afford the surgery.

Give me a break just this once."

Do you like to brag?

I must, because I do it a lot.

It seems to get the cobwebs out

And starts my journey to self-importance.

So I had told my patient and her mother,

I knew the best man for the job of mole removal.

And I can make the appointment right now.

Great surgeon, great with kids, he da man.

Now he had become not da man.

I had become da sucker.

Mom had became da victim

And the small patient charged to my care was in da middle.

Truth in advertising is a good slogan.

Mayo Clinic is a good brand.

Mike Wilson MD trained in dermatology there.

Thought he would put an advertisement in the paper.

You know: mention his training.

Mention his talent.

Mention his location.

Mention his great service in the care of dermatology.

There was a time where advertising in medicine was looked down on.

This was the time.

Mayo clinic said stop.

The local medical society said , "you are out."

Mike was and is a good doctor.

I had known that for a long time.

So I wrote a letter to the medical society.

Basically, "Come on man. This is America."

The medical society changed their mind.

Mayo Clinic backed off.

Everyone advertises now.

But Dr. Lock and I never needed to—too many patients.

My department chair in dermatology,

He cringed at the advertising,

He actually shrunk his whole visage when he saw a medical AD.

"Want to ruin medicine John? That should do it."

I have a friend in the Belgian Congo.

He is as white as the driven snow and Swedish to his soul.

Tried to come back to America.

"Can't do the profit thing. No fun. No action."

He made a family in the wild.

Two kids and a wife.

Snippets

They loved it too.

That's what I should have done.

That's what Mike, Dr. Lock, and all of us should have done.

Nothing says doctor like taking care of patients.

How lovely: no co-pays, no endless hassle of forms.

No endless insurance companies and drug companies to grovel to for patient assistance.

So things are like water.

They leave you with less.

So people are like the waterfall.

They leave you with more.

Dr. Lock never saw my patient.

The mother gracefully agreed to another surgeon.

I lost some credibility.

The biopsy was benign and the scar looked pretty damn good.

We got locked out.

The mother, the patient, and I.

168

Funny thing, Dr. Lock missed a great family.

He was locked out the most.

How about an advertisement:

"We see patients,

You come first,

No payments asked for but what you can spare.

You see the doctor everytime,

No medical assistant or nurse practioner will arbitrate your care.

You want to see the doctor.

The doctor wants to see you."

I have often thought of doing an AD just like that.

But I am locked in place.

Locked out of the best place anyone could be.

Locked.

The key, you must know by now, is in the shape of the cardioids.

Snippets

Drinking a Sprite

There is a club called "Righteous", rich white men, 50 strong.

I confess I am a member and white,

And rich compared to most of the world,

But my wealth is paltry compared to most in the group.

Breakfast.

"You know what I saw yesterday, John?

A HISPANIC lady at a McDonalds.

Asked for a free cup for water,

She then filled it with Sprite.

I accosted her of course.

She quickly disappeared.

The nerve, the nerve,

Can you believe there are people 'like that?'"

People "like that,!"

Hispanic.

Dishonest.

Poor and thirsty.

I did in fact know people like that.

And I have heard there are more than just a few.

My friend came from a family of great wealth,

And McDonalds would be one of the few places he could have met people "like that.!"

They are not dangerous.

They are truly of the nobility of the Hispanic.

They work hard.

They honor God and family.

It costs McDonalds less than a nickel.

Cup and all for an icy drink of Sprite.

No caffeine but lots of sugar.

Real energy pick up.

I also knew many people like my friend.

Always wanted to ditch them.

But never did.

Always wanted to tell them off.

I am not a brave man.

I am not one to often stick up for my fellow man.

I have a life to live.

I am, after all, I am a man of standing.

Breakfast was especially good that morning.

Orange juice, eggs, hashbrowns, bacon, pancakes.

Fruits of great variety.

All you could eat, even a Sprite.

My friend had a full plate.

Couldn't eat it all.

So he stacked the remains of the meal in a great refuse pile on the side of his plate.

He was stuffed full.

My minister says that breaking bread is an act of great friendship.

It means acceptance and respect for other.

Snippets

It offers time for conversation and bonding.

You have a chance to be at ease and congenial.

I like to imagine things.

I, as others, refer to them as "good visuals."

So I have had a "good visual" of breakfast.

The meal that gets the day off on the right foot.

Marshal Goodnight is not passing the bacon.

Marie Gonzalez is drinking a Sprite.

"Of all the nerve!" she says.

"Serving yourself the bacon and offering nothing to others."

Now a second scene:

My friend is old and will die soon.

"Nurse I could use a Sprite,

It once again is water. Take it from my lips!"

"Your hallucinating continues."

Visuals aren't necessarily real.

Hallucinating is not supposed to be real.

But it would sure taste good right now,

The refreshing sugary taste of a Sprite.

Paint

ROY G BIV, the rainbow of visible light.

Red, Orange, Yellow, Green, Blue, Indigo, Violet.

Violet, the shortest visible wave length.

Then comes invisible ultraviolet.

So I am going to paint everything violet.

It will take a very large paintbrush.

One with those long soft bristles.

So I can get into all the crevices.

Violet is the color of royalty.

Mary's robe was violet.

The violet flame, the Yin and Yang.

The color of the universe.

The Buddist and Hindu,

Violet is the color of the Crown Chakra.

Pure consciousness.

From which all Chakras eminate.

Martha Wakinyan was a brilliant physician.

She worked at the prestigious children's hospital in a large city.

The hospital said no part time work for a mother.

Her young children needed mother-time at home.

Martha quit.

She did not need the hospital.

They needed her.

She could build a peds derm practice on her own.

She seemed to know the most.

The most about pediatric dermatology.

The most of anyone I have ever known.

She had the best bedside manner.

So last Thursday, I got 2 frantic phone calls from mothers.

A child with molluscum spreading like wildfire.

A child with poison ivy spreading like wildfire.

My practice is too busy like wildfire.

So to put the fires out,

My secretary called Martha's office.

One child had insurance, "Send them right over."

One child did not, "Do not send."

So I saw the "Do not send child" at the end of my day.

Horrible poison ivy for 1 week.

Horrible nummular eczema for 8 months.

Mother so thankful, she wanted to cry.

She was beautiful.

She came with two little boys.

The patient, the youngest

The roundest, saddest, face I had ever seen.

He was in the year of six.

Children know everything.

There were heavy secrets behind those eyes.

His brother of eight stood sullenly by.

Did not want her to cry.

For something she deserved.

For something I was supposed to give.

For something we both needed.

Mom called three days later.

Son was much better.

"Thank God," she said.

She called from a battered women's shelter.

Martha and I started to walk across a great white paper.

It was Martha's medical record template,

We walked over office notes,

Patients' lists of allergies.

We walked across: who to call in an emergency.

Dates of immunizations.

Birthdates.

Past medical history.

We got to the top of the paper.

We crossed over a Cross,

This symbolized her medical group,

"Christian Physicians."

Just over the edge of the paper,

We saw the blue sky,

Middle of the day,

The sun shining brightly.

Suddenly a great paint brush

With soft quills

Painted everything violet.

The stationery, Martha, me, the Cross.

That was not all.

The sky was suddenly dipped in violet.

The sun gave off a violet hue.

Martha was gone.

There is something about the color violet.

There is a space between where we can and can't see.

I wonder where that is.

That space between violet and ultraviolet.

Someday I would like to go and see that space.

Maybe that is where Martha went.

To find something she left there in a crevice.

A crevice with no paint.

The Tambourine Lady

Well she shook her bright spangles.

And banged the worn rim

And most never noticed.

But God took her in.

Wore a neck brace of white

But could stand on her own.

To sounds of the songs

Her church hymnal sown.

Her rhythm was perfect

And I will confess

Only twice that a saw her

In church pews no less.

See her church was not my church.

Though she worshipped my God.

I attended so seldom

But can still hear her call.

Snippets

No beauty surpasses

Her faith it unfurls.

On Wednesday it's ashes.

Sunday: diamonds and pearls.

She said, "I will be with you:

In good times and bad,

In life and in death

Whether happy or sad."

So listen next morning.

When life has its start.

To the tambourine lady.

And the beat of her heart.

Killing the Snake

Scary things, snakes.

Two-headed, Nehebkau, guarded the underworld in Egyptian mythology.

Serpent snake in the Garden of Eden.

Could fool with hellish good rapport.

Evolutionary advantage for humans who feared snakes.

Easy to fear.

Slippery, slimey, hissing, deadly.

Curved slivery swish in the grass.

My gift: Talking off the cuff.

Off the wall.

About nothing.

In a way to impress you.

Aaaah, what a talent I have.

But, can you bullshit about medicine?

You can, you can.

My dear muse of the mouth.

My grades were good.

My exam grades OK.

Snippets

My volunteer activity list exemplary.

But the interview, serpentine and brilliant, tipped the scale for medical school admission.

Rachel Kingsley wanted,

In the worst way, in the hopeless way,

In the way of the snake,

To live to be a doctor.

Rachel was brilliant,

With the grades of a genius,

The test scores of the elite,

The heart of the angels.

She wanted to practice general medicine,

In a poor community.

Sometimes you know something

And I knew she could heal bodies as well as souls as few others.

But carried a coil around her neck.

She could not interview well.

So the missing gift of gab,

Would kill her dream.

Kill it like a club.

No admission committee could see past her great foible.

They would have to imagine her different.

Different than she appeared.

Coaching, no help.

Role-playing, not much better.

Clothing change was worth a try.

How could she manage patient care, the admission committees thought?

She volunteered with me at the free clinic.

Patients knew kindness.

I knew devotion.

Medicine would be better for her having step into the healing art.

Walking home from school,

In the grade of six,

Saw the enormous coil of orange,

String of red squares, lined in black.

Grab a stick, fear.

Pound it, pound it, pound it.

Until it stops writhing in pain.

Dead.

I think often of why I killed the snake.

I felt cold, sad, weak.

I found out later.

Corn snake, harmless eater of vermin, a creature of God.

You need to know what you are killing.

Before you take away a life.

Life and dreams are hard to come by.

They are the same, a gift that lasts forever.

The snake talks of eating apples.

Predictor of great success.

In the American Indian culture; death and rebirth.

Energy of integrity, achiever of wisdom.

Rachel's birthday of 26.

Still applying for medical school.

Not cheap but worth it she thought.

Could make it to interviews but not beyond.

The next day seemed like the next day.

But a letter in the mail said differently.

Acceptance.

She is aglow like the morning star.

Each wish is heard and seen by someone.

Each mirror reflects you.

Can you see the behind the mirror?

The good life behind what appears not so perfect.

But the snake is good. Symbolized the umbilical cord binding man to mother earth.

Medical symbol was the staff of Asclepius, demigod of medicine.

The Hopi Indians performed the snake dance to renew the fertility of nature.

Moses raised the snake as a sign of salvation.

Behold the noble snake, for He is the dual symbol of good and evil.

He lives, He lives!

I, the snake of deceit.

She, the snake of the truth

The medical school admissions.

They were not seen in the act of truth.

But I was seen on a summer afternoon,

Killing the snake.

They killed the snake of Devil.

I killed the snake of God.

Vietnam

I never wanted to write this story.

It is filled with man's taking of life.

It is filled with stupidity.

Stupidity for the art of healing.

It is filled with a lack of respect.

It is filled with courage coming up short.

With lack of follow through.

With lack of standard of care.

So I cannot be the doctor.

It hurts too much,

You are going to be the doctor,

You can endure the pain.

Drove by the Vietnam memorial this morning.

It is a beautiful day.

Can't drive by without thoughts.

Thoughts of Willie McCracken.

There are many strange diseases of the skin.

Pyoderma gangrenosum is one of them.

Harmless, life saving blood cell named the neutrophil.

It goes crazy.

Invades the skin like a swarm of killer bees,

Nothing left but a hole in the skin.

And masses of these once brave cells who saved its host by stamping out infection.

Nothing can stop them digging a hole through, skin, tendon, muscle.

It is not cancer.

It is just inflammation gone bezerk.

It is not infection, it is not gangrene.

It is a mass of pus eating to the bone.

The pain is beyond the pale,

The look defies logic.

The wound worsens sometimes over days.

The big guns of medicine must be brought in to save the mortal flesh.

Willie McCracken was the bravest man I have known.

Decorated multiple times in the jungles of Southeast Asia.

"Were you afraid?

You were wounded six times."

"Never afraid, I knew I would be OK."

Snippets

So there is a theory of genetics.

There may be a God gene.

People who believe in God survive better,

Because they think God is on their side.

Dean Hamer of the U.S. Cancer Institute has named it.

Written a book about it.

Vesicular monoamine transmitter 2(VMAT2) is increased.

Not a single theologian and few scientists agree.

An article written in a reputable medical journal,

It shows proof,

Scientifically quantitative proof,

The chemical in question unquestionalably are elevated.

It occurs to you, then, that Wille McCracken has the gene.

How could he be such an optimist?

"Let's write about it someday, Willie.

How you were never afraid."

"Sure Doc, helluva story."

"How are you doing now,

Trauma, depression? PTSD?"

"Not for me, living is great. Except for this leg."

Snippets

Lifts his pant leg,

20 by 8 inch ulcer on inner calf,

Deep to tendon,

Don't believe me? I have the photograph.

So pyoderma gangrenosum exhibits an enathema.

All ulcers heal better when debrided.

Debride pyoderma gangrenosum at your own risk.

You get pathergy—debridement makes it explode.

Look all day but don't touch!

The worst ulcer you will ever see.

But don't touch!

Do not graft; do not trim; do not remove the detritus!

Do not touch!

"The surgeon keeps cutting away at it,

He says it needs to be aggressively clean,

But it just keeps getting bigger."

"Tell him to STOP!"

Here is where phones, faxes, and computers fail you.

You have to tell the patient,

"Never see any surgeon for your leg again.

Never, ever let anyone touch your leg again."

You are a laid back doctor like me,

So you assume the obvious.

You are wrong,

All the angels in heaven cannot make you right.

Willie did not come for his visit in a month..

After 2 months I became concerned.

Called the wound care nurse.

Willie McCracken was dead.

"The surgeon kept debriding it weekly.

It got much worse.

It became infected.

He became septic and died."

You did it

You didn't stop the surgery.

He survived Vietnam.

But he couldn't survive you.

You can't write a book about bravery now.

You can write a book about incompetence.

And you can be the main character.

The main menace, the main tragedy.

The Vietnam Memorial in Kansas City is beautiful.

It has its own wall of honor.

Mimicking the one in D.C.

But smaller and seemingly more accesable with a beautiful fountain.

It's started raining.

But the Memorial is only 3 blocks from my office.

And I think a will drive by after work.

If it isn't too rainy, I will get out of my car.

Sit and think of those who died.

President Obama lifted the ban.

The ban on military weapons,

To be sent to the Vietnamese.

So how could so many have died for nothing?

Heard Daniel Ellsberg, of Pentagon Papers Fame, on NPR yesterday

Say "the war was murder."

You don't have to be in a war to commit murder.

Most would say it was miscalculation.

Snippets

The war in which I never served.

The patient whom I never saved.

Miscalculation? Murder? Sacrifice?

Saw a Vietnam Vet today.

He left friends in the jungle.

"It was all for nothing."

He said.

What was Vietnam?

The cold, black, wet obelisks stand at attention.

Some names are missing:

Robert McNamara, Lyndon Johnson,

Willie McCracken, and me.

Three do not belong.

I sure wish Willie was there.

I told you, I never wanted to write this story.

Routine

There is a friend and patient I see on repeated office visits.

193

He is 87 but in good health.

He is a clinical psychologist and is ok financially.

So I asked him, "why not retire?"

"I like the routine.

Getting up at the same time.

See my patients.

It gives me a reason.

The reason is the point.

It lets me be who I am.

It lets me see the world.

It lets the love of my patients be the order of the day."

Richard Q Crotty MD is the reason I am a skin doctor.

Always wanted to be like him.

Maybe I am.

He made a phone call that landed me a residency in dermatology.

What a guy he was,

Saw anyone who could make it in the door by 5:00 pm.

Patients jammed the waiting room. People lined the hallway

When his wits had left him, he left them with a hidden exit.

Snippets

He practiced at a time when patients won

Paper only, computers were nonexistent.

Big government and big insurance

Did not handcuff you to serve more secretary than MD.

I followed him around like a puppy for a month.

Loving his style.

His patient care.

His charisma.

Haven't thought of it for years

But every other Friday we left his office

And saw patients in a dingy office downtown.

Same care, same patients.

Now I know,

It was a free health clinic in Omaha.

All the dermatologists took there turns

Twice a month to see patients for free.

Only a pariah would avoid his turn.

It was expected.

It was an honor.

It was routine.

The 10 to 20 minutes for lunch

He napped on a narrow bench.

What a wimp I thought

But now I sleep in my chair over lunch.

So sometimes at night,

I wonder if I am as good as Dr. Crotty.

Saw him in a nursing home before he died.

Showed him a derm book I helped edit.

In the front of the book it was dedicated

"To Dr. Crotty who gave me a chance."

"Education, John, that is the key

That is what makes medicine great."

"I miss my wife," he said.

Through a mouth partially malshaped.

Malshaped by a recent stroke

But his smile looked perfect to me.

To me he looked exactly the same.

Too proud to be seen in his room.

He was wheeled in by a nurse.

Snippets

I fell back in time.

We were whirring from room to room.

"What do you think that was Johnny?

No, you're guessing, not looking at the patient.

Try looking at the patient."

Again, this morning,

I wonder if I lived up to his legacy.

Kept patients first,

And let the love of patients be the order of the day.

The free health clinic in my city

Currently has no dermatology volunteers but me.

I don't cover it adequately.

You are not looked down on if you don't participate.

Here is an oddity.

You are looked down on if you do participate.

"What a sucker,

You give away half your income anyway."

You give it to Medicare cuts.

You give it to insurance panel discounts.

You give to patients who can't pay in the office.

But it isn't quite the same.

I have occasionally contemplated:

If we paid doctors less or better yet poverty wages,

They would volunteer more

Volunteer doctors would have to take care of them.

Here would be the great benefit:

They could see what good free care is given by many in this country.

They could wear the true crown of gratefulness.

They might give their caregiver a gift---what a glorious sight.

Everyone who volunteers for free,

Like me, have found true freedom.

Freedom to be like Dr. Crotty.

Free to be routine .

The reason is the point.

It lets me be who I am.

It lets me see the world.

And the love of my patients be the order of the day.

A Walk on the Wild Side

So part of confession is weeding out the truth.

Or avoiding the truth.

Or being artful in omitting part of the truth.

Or just plain admitting when you're lying.

I lied this afternoon to a friend at lunch.

The worst kind of a lie.

I told him I was writing a few life stories,

But he wouldn't be in it.

So here I go putting him in.

He probably won't mind.

And I guess if you are a liar

You really don't care.

Discussing your innermost life is risky

But it usually doesn't stop me.

So here goes.

I confess I want to live on the wild side.

Most of life is between boring and not boring.

Snippets

But I want to go to the other possibility.

To live on the edge of the untamed.

Even if just for an afternoon.

The heat and humidity in the Midwest;

A killer.

I hate summer.

Reverse SAD.

SAD is really seasonal effective disorder.

Depressed in the winter.

Treat with sun-mimicking lights.

A trip to the Bahamas.

Mine is reverse.

Depressed in summer.

Sun triggers migraines.

Humidity triggers claustrophobia.

Treat with cold, dark house.

Trip to the mountains.

But here is the best:

Lunch with Mr. Rettun.

Snippets

Mr. Rettun.

Most humanitarian of all humans.

Gives support to every good cause.

Can make me laugh on the muggiest of days.

I really have the ability, if you call it that.

To become depressed any time.

The glory of genetics.

My mother was the source.

Should have been more sympathetic to her.

But a depressed hostile person is hard to love.

I did love her but less than I should have.

But I was the one to receive the curse.

So here is a way to solve the deeps.

The deeps is the commonest malady.

According to WHO,

To cause significant morbidity in the world.

Over extend.

Throw in a little exhaustion.

Find a cause.

And overdue it a bit.

Takes you out of yourself.

Makes you a cowboy.

Purpose bridges the deeps.

Live on the side of the cliff.

I know a cardiologist.

I can always be jealous.

They make about a million a year.

But I think he ventured into the depths also.

Always tempting fate.

Skiing in the best resorts.

Hiking to base camp at Mount Everest.

Left to live in the mountains.

Great guy.

Great wife.

Great family.

I have all that too, sans great guy.

But I need a little off the chart too.

So I find it at lunch.

Yes, lunch.

Snippets

That great invention of true psychiatry.

I love to eat with friends at lunch.

Really only have time on Fridays.

Too busy playing Roy Rogers.

"The King of the Cowboys."

When I was a kid I had the whole outfit.

Chaps, fringed vest, holster with a silver gun.

Great looking official Roy Roger's boots.

And the Stetson hat of the range.

My gloves had fringes too.

A twenty pound terrier

Noticed me trying to get into the car after school.

I am sure stalking me for days.

That monstrous animal,

I feared dogs anyway,

Grabbed the fringes of a glove.

And ran off in triumph into the wild.

My mother saw the whole thing.

She was furious.

These cowboy authentics were not cheap.

Even I was a little aghast at the cowardice of Roy Rogers.

So time off is often not a friend.

And I take some Fridays away from my practice.

So I tantalize close to the underground

Until lunch.

I know what you're thinking

Mr. Rettun who is a businessman of great means,

Will fly us to France for lunch on the Riveiera.

We might stop off at the Louvre on our way north.

The great vacation spots of the world,

To be wild you must be different,

Who would want a common meal in the Swiss Alps?

Anyone with a few million could do that.

Our monthly noon meals are in the modest office of Mr. Rettun.

He lives in a modest house

He has a modest lifestyle.

But we do not have a modest lunch.

To get to his office,

You must walk by virtually every award given in our city

For support of charities large and less large.

Snippets

People trying to sustain a better life for all.

We are served in his small very modest conference room

By two of the great people in our lives.

They cater us as if we are royalty.

The food is superb.

Canned salmon from Alaska.

Fresh peaches from the Omish orchards.

Meat from the best sources in the world.

Dates from the Orient.

But the best foods are from his secretary's garden and locally bought candies.

And the best diet root beer the corner grocery can sell.

Then we spend two hours solving not just our world

But solving for all the universe, forever.

We end with a hug.

I feel the elevator pull me from the depths,

God has taught me once again, as my minister says,

Relationship is everything.

Take that queen of England.

Take that Donald Trump.

Take that cardiology.

Snippets

Take that depression.

So if you're looking for me on Friday afternoon

I might be at lunch

Walking on the wild side.

God bless the wildness in us all.

Grace

I do a lot more sleeping these days.

I'm older.

It's an escape.

I don't notice the headaches then.

They might be there.

I might dream about them.

But after awhile, when I wake,

The pain is gone.

Snippets

My son says he read this about migraines.

They come from an unresolved conflict.

I know what it is but don't like to admit it.

It could be because I am wrong about it.

I'm an imposter.

That is the main problem.

I am supposed to be someone else.

My brain and my God know this.

My friends and my family mostly don't know this.

But some have figured it out.

I am glad they did.

It makes things easier.

Have you ever thought you might be living the wrong life?

You just got turned around,

And before you know it,

You awaken and you are someone else.

Snippets

I am supposed to be an English professor.

All my friends in grade school, high school, college,

They all know this.

They know that is what I would be the best at doing.

The students were to be my lifelong fellows in life.

My parents and siblings knew it too.

I was to be a teacher of great import.

A master of subject and pupil.

The teacher of the year, the decade, the century.

Admired by all for my great empathy.

For my great caring.

For my unsurpassed creativity.

My students were to love me.

They fight for their children to take my class.

In old age they would come back to see me.

To tell me of their love and admiration.

I changed their lives.

I made them better people.

I gave them the chance to be.

To be the best that they could be.

So they say that with age my headaches will fade.

But now I am that age.

They are with me still.

My son has read correctly.

So I am about to go to sleep.

To leave the throbbing behind once again.

When I open my eyes, maybe I will be who I was supposed to be.

Maybe things will be as they should be.

I won't be out for money.

I won't be out for me.

I will be out for others.

My God will be proud of me.

The people who I thought they would look up to me,

Snippets

They will look up to see the face they knew would show up.

The person I was meant to be.

They knew it all along.

No war in Vietnam.

No struggle to reinvent myself.

No stranger that I live with.

No brain on fire.

Only quiet.

Only calm.

Only sleep to rest.

Only peace.

So I am bleeding on the page.

The wound is open.

It festers still.

It will not heal.

I wish to you and yours no pain.

Only to be what you are supposed to be.

That should be enough.

Enough for no headaches before and after you go to sleep.

My wife of 48 years,

She says I am supposed to be this.

A healer of wounds.

Could she know a thing or two?

You can never know.

But I have found it hard to argue.

Hard to argue with a woman.

A woman of compelling faith.

And when the day is done.

When the last patient has left me their story.

I know she is right after all.

It is the privilege of a lifetime.

To be a part of someone else's life.

It must be viewed as hallowed ground.

Where people share

Their hope, faith, pain, and love.

The headaches are gone.

God has given me grace.